S0-AAF-849

STUDENT SUCCESS MODELING

STUDENT SUCCESS MODELING:

Elementary School to College

Edited by
Raymond V. Padilla

Foreword by Sarita E. Brown

STERLING, VIRGINIA

Sty/us

COPYRIGHT © 2009 BY STYLUS PUBLISHING, LLC.

Published by Stylus Publishing, LLC
22883 Quicksilver Drive
Sterling, Virginia 20166-2102

All rights reserved. No part of this book may be reprinted or
reproduced in any form or by any electronic, mechanical or
other means, now known or hereafter invented, including
photocopying, recording and information storage and
retrieval, without permission in writing from the publisher.

xix + 212 p.

$69.95
$29.95

Library of Congress Cataloging-in-Publication-Data
Student success modeling : elementary school to college /
edited by Raymond V. Padilla.
   p.   cm.
   Includes bibliographical references and index.
   ISBN 978-1-57922-326-7 (cloth : alk. paper)—
   ISBN 978-1-57922-327-4 (pbk. : alk. paper)
   1. School improvement programs—United States—Case
studies.   2. Students—United States—Case studies.
3. Success—United States—Case studies.   4. Children with
social disabilities—Education—United States—Case
studies.   I. Padilla, Raymond V.
LB2822.82.S843   2009
371.200973—dc22   2008025786

13-digit ISBN: 978-1-57922-326-7 (cloth)
13-digit ISBN: 978-1-57922-327-4 (paper)

Printed in the United States of America

All first editions printed on acid free paper
that meets the American National Standards Institute
Z39-48 Standard.

Bulk Purchases

Quantity discounts are available for use in workshops
and for staff development.
Call 1-800-232-0223

First Edition, 2009

10   9   8   7   6   5   4   3   2   1

To all students who succeeded and to those who helped them along the way, because success is achieved one student at a time.

CONTENTS

FIGURES

ACKNOWLEDGMENTS

I appreciate the interest and hard work of several generations of graduate students who were intrepid enough to work with evolving ideas that were still hatching in my mind. Their work compelled me to rethink over and over again the basic ideas that now frame the Expertise Model of Student Success (EMSS). Michael Pavel was there from the beginning. I learned from the work of Louis Attinasi, Jr., and Monica Lowe. Other graduate students from Arizona State University included Robert Fallows, Joseph Saggio, Sylvia Melchior-Walsh, and Romero Jalomo. Jesus Treviño, a former undergraduate student with a doctorate from UCLA, encouraged me to return to EMSS after a lapse of several years. Kenneth Gonzalez became an advocate of EMSS after he became a faculty member. At the University of Texas at San Antonio, a new generation of graduate students contributed important work that finally allowed me to bring this volume together. They include Kimberly Barker, Mary Miller, Ralph Mario Wirth, George Norton, and Lana Myers. Some of their work is included in this book. I am grateful for all their hard work. I am also grateful to the University of Texas at San Antonio for the sabbatical leave that made preparing the book less daunting.

T oday's global economy is knowledge based. The level of math required to be a production associate in an automobile plant is higher than that possessed by half of the 17-year-olds in the United States. Approximately 90 percent of the high-growth occupations in the United States require some postsecondary education or training, and the U. S. Bureau of Labor predicts that the number of jobs requiring science, engineering, or technical training will rise by 24 percent between 2004 and 2014.

The Nation's Report Card, more formally known as the National Assessment of Educational Progress (NAEP), is a congressionally mandated task undertaken by the U.S. Department of Education to evaluate the condition of education in the nation. In 2005 a representative sample of over 21,000 high school seniors from 900 schools across the country was assessed in reading and mathematics. The report for that year underscores the need for greater academic achievement for all U.S. students as judged by their performance on NAEP. It also emphasizes the ethnic and racial divide in academic achievement and in college preparedness in both reading and mathematics. More specifically, the results indicated that reading performance declined for all but top performers. The percentage of students performing at or above the *Basic* level decreased from 80 percent in 1992 to 73 percent in 2005, and the percentage of students performing at or above the *Proficient* level decreased from 40 to 35 percent. In mathematics, White students scored higher than their Black and Hispanic counterparts, and the score gaps between White and Black students and White and Hispanic students were relatively unchanged since 1992.

Another yardstick of academic progress is college readiness—the level of preparation that students need in order to succeed in credit-bearing coursework at associate and baccalaureate degree granting institutions. Looking at ACT data for 2005, only half of the ACT tested high school graduates were ready for college, and 33 percent of the Latina/o students, the fastest growing population in the country, demonstrated their readiness to handle the reading requirements for typical credit-bearing first-year college coursework (ACT, 2006).

Educators and policy makers are working to improve overall student achievement at all levels of the educational system and to attain parity among ethnic and racial groups while the United States navigates its place in the world. Thirty-five years ago, more than half of the science and engineering doctorates in the entire world were earned in the United States. The National Bureau of Economic Research expects that share to fall to 15 percent by the year 2010. Other countries are gaining ground, according to several national academies, while "the scientific and technical building blocks of our economic leadership are eroding" (Committee on Prospering in the Global Economy of the 21st Century: An Agenda for American Science and Technology, National Academy of Sciences, National Academy of Engineering, and Institute of Medicine, 2007, p. 68).

Patrick Callan (2005), president of the National Center for Public Policy and Higher Education, agrees:

> The United States is not number one in the world anymore in higher education, in terms of proportion of people who go to college. We were flat for the whole decade, while England, France, Ireland, Spain, all had double digit increases. Why? Because they figured out that whoever succeeds in the development of human talent, whoever wins the educational sweepstakes, is going to have a huge advantage in the economic competition.

For the United States to remain competitive, its population—which will comprise a greater proportion of students of color, immigrant students, and the first in their family to go to college—must be not just educated, but also well educated. This is not news; it is oft repeated. Yet, despite the consensus of opinion about the critical importance of a highly functional P–20 educational system, these assessments have failed to catalyze direct investment in new tactics and powerful strategies to capture this talent and to serve all students well.

Today, as never before, the call for higher productivity and better educational outcomes dominates public policy discussions. The growing recognition of the critical importance of the country's human capital and the pressing need to improve educational outcomes is making its way into the media and the thoughts and concerns of the general public. So how is the educational system responding? By working hard to continue to do what it knows how to do, while acknowledging the mismatch between society's needs and the outcomes produced by the current system and practices.

Educators formally trained in their disciplines work in organizational structures and rely on models and tools designed to quantify failures rather than to support success—until now. *Student Success Modeling: Elementary School to College* delivers a new set of tools just in time. While thoughtfully explaining why most educational research emphasizes failure, this book quickly moves to a new Expertise Model of Student Success (EMSS) with its attendant Local Student Success Model (LSSM) and shows how to use these models to discover the means to support and accelerate student success. The authors provide the means to "answer the question that is being asked, not the one that is most familiar and tractable" (Padilla, this volume [p. 15]). The ideas and strategies offered in this book provide educators with powerful tools to respond to the driving question to be answered in the coming years—how will the United States tap the current generation of college-going students?

In writing this foreword, I follow the lead offered by the contributors to this book in their "autoethnographic encounters." My vantage point is from a national, educational, nonprofit organization whose aim is to accelerate student success in higher education for the country's fastest growing population, the Latina/o community. Since 2004 *Excelencia* in Education has worked to distill available information on the status of Latina/o access, persistence, and achievement in higher education to discern points of intervention and effective strategies and tactics to accelerate Latina/o student success. We join the ranks of other organizations working hard to better serve today's students as they become tomorrow's workers and leaders. We welcome this book and the promise of the ideas and models offered to educators in our schools, colleges, and universities. With *Student Success Modeling* as a guide, educators will be able immediately to construct learning approaches that break through the limitations of current large-scale assessments and build on all students' potential for success.

Improving educational outcomes now may mitigate a predicted shortage of 12 million college-educated workers in the United States by the year 2020. These statistics are staggering. Armed with the enhanced ability to focus on success offered by this book and with strategic investments of time, political will, and money well spent, the United States could harness the energy of millions of college-bound students who are eager to enrich America's future.

Sarita E. Brown
President
Excelencia in Education

References

ACT. (2006). *Ready to succeed: All students prepared for college and work.* Retrieved May 24, 2008 from http://www.act.org/research/policymakers/pdf/ready_to_succeed.pdf

Callan, P. (2005). *Declining by degrees: Higher education at risk.* Retrieved May 24, 2008 from http://www.decliningbydegrees.org/meet-experts-6-transcript.html

Committee on Prospering in the Global Economy of the 21st Century: An Agenda for American Science and Technology, National Academy of Sciences, National Academy of Engineering and Institute of Medicine. (2007). *Rising above the gathering storm: Energizing and employing America for a brighter future.* Retrieved May 24, 2008 from http://www.nap.edu/catalog/11463.html#toc

Padilla, R. V. (2008). Chapter 1, this volume (p. 15).

U.S. Department of Education, Institute of Education Sciences, National Center for Education Statistics. (2005). *National Assessment of Educational Progress (NAEP), 2005 mathematics assessment.* Retrieved May 25, 2008 from http://nationsreportcard.gov/reading_math_grade12_2005/s0307.asp?subtab_id = Tab_2&tab_id = tab1#chart

B y the second half of the ninteenth century, the United States had already moved inexorably into the industrial age, leaving behind the agricultural life of previous generations. While agricultural workers needed little or no formal schooling, the new industrial age demanded more skilled and better-educated workers. Workers needed to acquire at least the rudiments of reading, writing, and arithmetic if the industrial machines and the organizations that operated them were to be sustained and made profitable. Even those workers toiling on factory floors and later on assembly lines needed the benefits of basic schooling so that they could stay healthy, go to work on time, follow directions, value honesty and hard work, and discharge effectively their civic responsibilities. Thus arose the demand for free, public (and even compulsory) education for everyone.

Before the state took an interest in public education there were already three pedagogical questions of long standing: What is to be taught? How can it be taught effectively? What determines a student's success? Philosophers, pedagogues, religious instructors, and even parents had wrestled for many centuries and in many places with these basic questions. However, these and similar questions had to be asked all over again in the new context of universal public education where students from many walks of life would be taught by the millions. It is only a bit ironic that the industrial age produced education on an industrial scale. So the fundamental questions related to education had to be asked anew in the context of mass education, education that literally was built on industrial processes and ways of thinking. In hindsight, one can see that mass education was both a product and a driver of the industrial age.

This book focuses on one of the key questions: What determines a student's success? While this appears to be a simple question to understand, it is not so easy to answer. It is especially not so easy to answer in a holistic and comprehensive manner. Like the proverbial blind men trying to characterize an elephant from one of its parts, thinkers of various sorts often have tried to answer the question by generalizing from a small part or a specific context to the whole of student success. This book makes the case that we need to develop general models of student success that also can be applied locally to specific situations and contexts so that we can achieve both generality and specificity. Moreover, the general and local models ought to be able to help educators to enhance student success.

The general model followed in this book is the Expertise Model of Student Success (EMSS), which can be instantiated at a specific school as a local student success model (LSSM). These models can be applied to almost any educational setting and level. Once developed, the LSSM can be used to take actions that may help students to be more successful. Clearly, other models need to be developed as well so that in the long run educators and the public at large can choose the model they deem most appropriate. So far, general models of student success have been lacking, and researchers need to redouble efforts to generate new ones and improve those that already exist.

Chapter 1 presents the general problem of student educational outcomes and how researchers have tried to grapple with it. In particular, it is important to distinguish between research that examines student dropout and studies that focus on student success. Chapter 2 presents the Expertise Model of Student Success in detail. It includes a discussion of both the conceptual foundations and the research methods used in the model. Chapters 3 through 6 are contributed chapters that are based on the doctoral research of former students who took an interest in EMSS. In chapter 3 Mary Miller reports on a comparative study of a high-performing and a non-high-performing elementary school using EMSS as a tool for comparison. In chapter 4 Kimberly Barker writes about her study of student success at the high school level, in which valuing education is a central finding. In the following chapter, Ralph Wirth reports on his study of student success at a still emerging community college with a student-centered mission. In chapter 6 Padilla and George Norton report on research in progress related to student success at a Hispanic Serving Institution. These chapters can be seen as examples of doing research with EMSS from the elementary school level to postsecondary education. The slight variations in the treatment and display of data show the reader how EMSS can be used flexibly and creatively.

Chapter 7 focuses on the practical aspects of EMSS in terms of taking action to improve student success. This chapter will be of interest to those who have the responsibility to promote student success and who are looking for tools to get the job done. The last chapter revisits some of the issues presented in chapter 1 and calls for expanding the conversation on student success, now that we are finally turning the corner, by focusing on success instead of nonsuccess or failure. Most of the chapters contain an "Autoethnographic Encounter." These texts narrate personal experiences that provide additional insights into the issues that are otherwise covered in the book in a more academic style. While there are a considerable number of citations in the book, the intent is to make the material accessible to a wide range of readers who are interested in student educational outcomes.

I

THE PREOCCUPATION WITH
STUDENT OUTCOMES

Student success is an outcome of human interaction in complex educational systems, which in turn are embedded in complex social systems. Although success is one important outcome, there are a number of ways in which student outcomes can be considered (see Figure 1.1). For example: What is the level of students' satisfaction with their schooling or collegiate experience? Do students stay in school or drop out?. More generally, what is each student's ongoing progress (e.g., grades) and eventual graduation status? Some social scientists have looked at outcomes as the impact of schooling and college on, for example, students' lifetime income, political attitudes, socioeconomic status, or intergenerational educational attainment. Still others examine educational outcomes from the perspective of graduate study enrollment rates and career impacts. Clearly, the interest in student outcomes is high and encompasses a range of concerns.

Figure 1.1 attempts to bring some order to these and related perspectives by separating those perspectives that relate to student performance from all others. Under the category of student performance, four subcategories have been well covered in the research literature: studies related to dropouts (departure), retention, persistence, and student success. Unfortunately, the boundaries between these subcategories are not always clear. Additional confusion is created when research approaches are brought into the picture. Many studies are descriptive, correlational, or based on general constructs borrowed from the social sciences. In contrast, other studies offer actual models or theories that apply specifically to dropping out or to student success.

FIGURE 1.1
Concept Model of Research on Student Outcomes

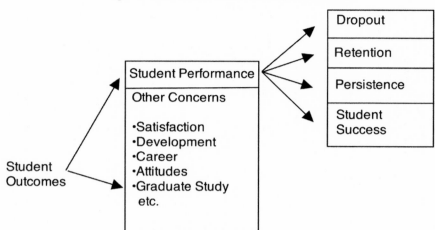

Figure 1.2 makes an effort to sort through the various types of student performance studies and to show the relationships that connect them. The model has two major axes: The horizontal axis represents student persistence and nonpersistence, while the vertical axis represents student retention or lack thereof. Quadrant I is the domain of research related specifically to student success models. In this quadrant student retention is a precondition to success, as is persistence. A student who is retained is still registered at some specific point in time. If the student persists, the student is retained for a continuous period of time. If the length of time is sufficient and the student has met graduation requirements, then persistence becomes graduation.

Quadrant II represents retention and persistence studies that do not use complete models of student success. Rather, they may be descriptive or correlational studies. In some cases they may borrow specific constructs or general theories from the social sciences to frame the research. These studies are distinguishable from those in quadrant I in that they do not offer a complete model of student success that is theoretically grounded and empirically testable.

The research in quadrant III represents substantial models of student dropout. Here the most commonly recognized model is Tinto's model of college student departure. As are student success models, student dropout models

FIGURE 1.2
A Concept Model of Research on Student Performance Outcomes

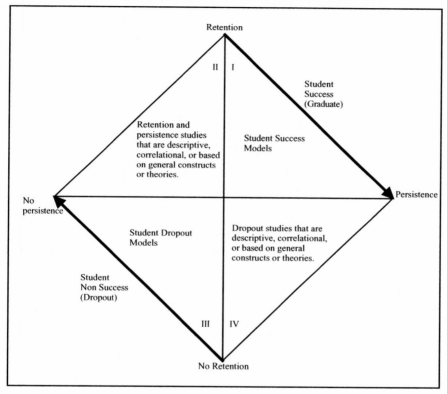

are theoretically based and empirically testable. It is clear from Figure 1.2 that student success models are different in kind from student dropout models. Still, perhaps because of the historic emphasis on dropout models and the more recent emphasis on student success models, some authors tend to blur the distinction between the two approaches, which can easily confuse those new to the field. As shown in Figure 1.2, a dropout is a student who has not been retained at a certain point in time and whose persistence is thus terminated.

Quadrant IV is the location of dropout studies that are descriptive or correlational. Also included are studies that may borrow constructs or general theories from the social sciences. These studies do not provide comprehensive models of student dropout. As can be seen from the figure, quadrant

IV studies have a relationship to quadrant III studies that is analogous to the relationship between studies in quadrants II and I.

In this book we take a rather simple approach to student success. A student is experiencing success when he or she is progressing satisfactorily through a program of study, and the student and others expect that the student will complete the program of study, resulting in either promotion to the next level or graduation. Graduation is still an important element of student success; however, some would relax that requirement, arguing that in some cases the goal of the student is what matters. If a student, for example, matriculates in a community college for the purpose of completing a few job-related courses or a vocational program that does not result in the associate degree, then such a student can be seen as successful even if no degree is awarded. Moreover, some students can take considerably longer than four years to graduate from college. Other students can swirl in their enrollment patterns, registering either serially or in parallel across institutions. However, we have chosen the more traditional view of success that includes satisfactory progress and graduation, because parents, policy makers, and educators all value graduation as an indicator of student success. Students as well place a high value on graduation. However, in certain contexts a broader view of success may be appropriate.

The Significance of Scale and Complexity

Student success occurs in the context of mass education. It is easy to lose sight of the huge number of students who must be educated in a large nation. According to the National Center for Education Statistics (2004), public elementary and secondary school enrollment in the United States was estimated at 48 million in 2003 and projected to reach 49.7 million by 2013. In 2002, 56.1 percent of the U.S. population between the ages of 3 and 34 was enrolled in school. To support such large-scale education requires massive amounts of resources. The federal government alone spent $166.1 billion in education during 2006 through the activities of more than 10 departments and agencies (NCES, 2006). This figure does not include the educational expenditures of the 50 states and hundreds of school districts throughout the country that depend heavily on property taxes. Many of these school districts have substantial operating budgets. A local school district in a large city in the Southwest recently announced that its proposed annual operating budget was nudging toward the one-billion-dollar mark, coming in at over $900 million from all sources. This is a significant investment that gets repeated across the nation in large, urban school districts. In light of such large numbers of students and such large dollar amounts, promoting student success also must be seen on a large scale—an important contextual factor to keep in mind, because increased success is needed for millions of students, not just a few of them.

After quantity, complexity enters the picture (Dörner, 1989; Stehr, 1992). The act of teaching and learning is embedded in multiple and cross-cutting layers of organization, control, and influence. A model of student success must be linked to additional models of other important processes that surround core educational activities. The entire suite of models can be thought of as "conjugate models" that together account for the stability and change of educational practices and outcomes. Figure 1.3 shows how such conjugate models might come together into a more or less cohesive but certainly complex whole.

The figure shows that education occurs within the "life world" diamond of everyday affairs, where people attend to the business of living. This life world is driven by the horizontal dimension of evaluation, which influences values, attitudes, and actions in everyday life. Most ordinary people are interested in the value of what they are doing either for the present or for the future. They will tend to support what they consider to be valuable activities and shun what they think is of little or no value. The second dimension that drives the life world is related to cognition and conation. Cognition takes into account the mental or psychological aspects of human behavior, while conation focuses on action or the will to act. At the end of the day, a decision has to be made, even if the decision is to do nothing. The life world and the issues processed therein (education, for example) thus are driven by cognitive states and dispositions, evaluative judgments, and the will to act. Clearly, there is much complexity in this scenario.

To bring some order into this complex arena, we can devise various models for specific components that tend to stand out. Broadly speaking, there are two models on the cognitive side and another two models on the conative side. The cognitive models include a policy model and a theoretical model. The hallmark of the policy model is politics, which can be seen as driven by ideology and resources. For any given issue in the life world (including education), the policy model will determine the ideological framework that will drive action and the level of resources that will be allocated to

FIGURE 1.3
Conjugate Models as the Drivers of Systematic Action in a Complex Life World

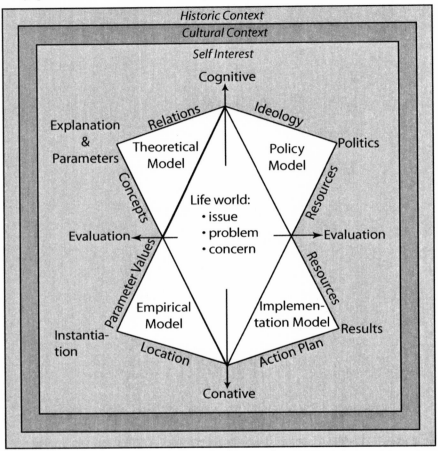

address the issue. All along, evaluative considerations will be in play within a political context. The theoretical model, on the other hand, has explanation and the specification of parameters as its hallmarks. This model signals the scientific or rational understanding of things. It is driven by a set of concepts that can be tied together with a set of relationships to explain a particular phenomenon in the life world. The theoretical model must be specific enough so that those who use it know what to look for and even measure as they try to use the model. Through observations and measurements, the theoretical model can be made explicit and applied in specific life-world contexts. For any given theoretical model, evaluative concerns are expressed by the academic community that strives to establish the value and worthiness of the model.

The two conative models include empirical and implementation models. The empirical model is closely related to the theoretical model. The major difference is that the empirical model takes the general theoretical model and applies it to a specific situation or location. The parameters identified in the theoretical model are given explicit values based on observations and measurements made in a given location. This kind of specification of a theoretical model based on empirical data or observations is called an *instantiation* of the theoretical model; that is, the empirical model represents an instance of the theoretical model. Clearly, while there is only one theoretical model, it may be instantiated at many locations over time. Evaluative arguments enter into the discussion of empirical models, regarding accuracy of measurements, appropriateness of data collection and analysis, the relevance of the theoretical model being instantiated, and many other similar concerns.

The implementation model focuses on results and is driven by some kind of action plan and the allocation of resources. The implementation model is necessarily contextualized within the other three models, for it always depends on the prevailing policy, theoretical, and empirical models to give it weight and justification. While one or more of these models may not be well developed or remain implicit, they will nonetheless affect the nature and quality of the implementation model. The hallmark of the implementation model is results. After money, time, and effort are spent on some activity, almost everyone wants to know if the results are satisfactory. This is where evaluative considerations come into the discussion of implementation models: Did we succeed or fail?

The use of conjugate models can be seen as one way to rein in some of the complexity of the life world. Such models are in a high state of mutual interaction, making it impossible to stay within one model and ignore the others. To further complicate matters, the models as a whole are contextualized within a set of metainfluences: self-interest, culture, and historical evolution. All of these models are affected by the interests of those who promote or oppose them. Those with greater resources and influence may see their interests prevail as the models are crafted and implemented. The poor and the powerless may get short changed. The models may be influenced also by collective interests that can be expressed in political and cultural terms. Models are developed always in a particular cultural context that involves religion, language, social norms, customs, traditions, and so on. In a society marked by extensive cultural diversity, the impact of culture may be significant in determining which models are established, recognized, and valued. Cultural minorities may have a difficult time having their voices heard. Thus, one must always be on the lookout for ethnocentrism in the construction of the various models. Finally, all models are developed within a historic context. Societies evolve over time, so models tend to reflect the evolution of a society up to a given point. As the society continues to evolve, the nature of the models may change along with it. Many of the problems dealt with in the life world have at their roots the obsolescence of extant models, models no longer applicable due to historic evolution and societal change. The key issue then is to determine what the new models should be like.

The chief purpose of Figure 1.3 is to demonstrate the complexity of the context in which student success is to be studied and understood. But it also can serve to signal to the reader that in this book the main focus is on the two left-hand models, namely the theoretical and the empirical models. Thus, the Expertise Model of Student Success (EMSS) that is the main subject of this book is a theoretical model that presents a particular understanding of student success by bringing together a set of concepts and the relationships that connect them. The EMSS then can be used to develop *local student success models* (LSSMs) that are based on empirical observations at a particular school or campus. These LSSMs are instantiations of the Expertise Model of Student Success. The LSSMs in turn can be used to drive implementation models to promote student success on a particular campus. However, as shown by the conjugate models drawing, any implementation model of necessity is also built on policy models that can range from those of the local governing board to those of the state legislature and the U.S. Congress. It is of little wonder that promoting student success is a difficult and challenging task that involves large numbers and complex phenomena.

Student Success in Perspective

While today it has become increasingly popular to focus on student success at all levels of the educational system, it is ironic that most of the historic research emphasizes not student success but lack of success. Throughout the second half of the twentieth century, scholars and practitioners attempted to determine what accounts for the departure of students from schools and colleges before they complete their programs of study and graduate. To that end, many quantitative and qualitative studies, along with numerous interventions, were implemented to prevent students from dropping out. But knowing why students leave school or college prematurely is not the same as knowing what accounts for student success. Student success involves more than preventing students from abandoning their studies. To promote student success one also must understand why many students, some of them under the most challenging circumstances, are able to complete all program requirements and actually graduate with a diploma or degree. If one can understand how it is that such students achieve their success, one can develop strategies and practices that will enable more students to perform as the successful ones do. So while the emphasis on dropouts can drive departure prevention strategies, the emphasis on success promotes enabling strategies that can lead students to academic progress and, ultimately, graduation.

Given the traditional research emphasis on dropouts, it may be useful to summarize the key approaches that have been used to study the subject. This will provide a means to see more clearly the differences between approaches that focus on dropouts and those that emphasize student success. Recently, a review of the dropout literature focusing on higher education was provided by Kuh and colleagues (Kuh, Kinzie, Buckley, Bridges, & Hayek, 2006). Table 1.1 outlines a taxonomy, influenced by these authors, of approaches to the study of dropouts.

As already noted, studying why students drop out does not necessarily lead to understanding how students stay and achieve. Student success can be seen as involving two closely related facets: Students must progress steadily through their program of study, and they must complete it to graduate. The first facet has received some attention in the research literature, although not as extensive as that devoted to dropouts. Following the analysis conducted by Ralph Wirth (2006), Table 1.2 summarizes the approaches that researchers have used in an effort to understand why students do progress through their studies.

Encouraged by foundation and other support, the first approach, student effort and engagement, in recent years has become widespread as surveys of student engagement are conducted across the country at both the

TABLE 1.1
Major Research Approaches Used to Study College Dropouts

Approach	Exemplars	Notes
Integrationist	Tinto (1987); etc.	Theoretical roots are sociological and tap into Durkheim's theory of suicide. They are also anthropological to the extent that they tap into Van Gennep's rites of passage as a key aspect of college integration. Key to this approach is the idea that students must integrate into the academic and social culture on campus if they are to continue their studies and not leave prematurely. Widely recognized as the predominant approach to the study of college dropouts during the last half of the 20th century.
Intentional	Bean (1983); etc.	Based on the employee turnover model. Departure is seen as an intentional act based on the individual's assessment of fit within the organization. Those students who intend to drop out because of the lack of fit with the campus will tend to drop out in fact.
Psychological Traits	Astin (1984); Bean & Eaton (2000); Dweck (2000); Kuh (1999); Rousseau (1995); etc.	Psychological constructs and theories are used to explain why students drop out. Such constructs include self-efficacy, locus of control, self-theories, motivational theory, psychological contract theory, etc.
Cultural Traits	Attinasi, Jr. (1986); Kuh & Love (2000); Lowe (1989); Melchior-Walsh (1994); Nora (2004); Rendón, Jalomo, & Nora (2000); Tierney (1993); etc.	Cultural incompatibilities along with issues of racism, discrimination, and assimilationist ideology are seen as affecting student dropout decisions. Can incorporate cultural critiques and constructs such as cultural and social capital as analytic tools.
Economic	Braxton (2003); Goldin, Katz, & Kuziermko (2006); St. John, Cabrerra, Nora, & Asker (2000)	Relies on cost-benefit analysis to explain why students may choose to leave college. When the student perceives that costs exceed benefits, then the student may be disposed to abandon college study in favor of alternate and more beneficial activities.

Citations are illustrative.

community college and four-year-college levels. The information gathered through these surveys is supposed to be used by college personnel to promote student engagement and thus encourage their success. According to Wirth, research on the identification of barriers and obstacles to student progress can be summarized as shown in Table 1.3.

TABLE 1.2
Major Approaches Used to Study Student Academic Progress

Approach	Exemplars	Notes
Student effort and engagement	Chickering & Gamson (1987); CCSSE (2004, 2005, 2007); Friedlander et al. (1990); Kuh, Pace, & Vesper (1997); Pace (1984); etc.	Has roots in Pace's concept of the student's level of effort that was subsequently expanded to the concepts of student engagement and involvement.
Student satisfaction	Ahrens & Boatwright (1997); Bilsky (2000); Borglum (1998); etc.	Students continue their studies when they are generally satisfied with their college; however, there can be some tolerance for dissatisfaction based on the desirability of receiving a degree or credential.
Persistence	Bourdon & Carducci (2002); Cofer & Somers (2000); Fallows (1987); Rowland (2003); Saggio (2000); Tinto (2000); White (2004); etc.	Largely correlational or descriptive studies that attempt to find links between individual or environmental variables and a student's continued enrollment.
Overcoming obstacles or barriers	Hilliard (2003); Kazis & Liebowitz (2003); Padilla & Pavel (1986); etc.	Student-centered perspective that attempts to identify campus-specific barriers that students must overcome to continue their studies.
Resilience	Garza, Reyes, & Trueba (2004); Gordon (1996); McMillan & Reed (1994); etc.	Looks for individual attributes and environmental factors that contribute to student progress and success in spite of serious challenges and obstacles.

Citations are illustrative.
After Wirth (2006).

Needless to say, there also are many ways in which student progress can be assessed using specific indicators, such as grade-point average, selection of a major, the number of credits accumulated, meeting specific program requirements, and so on. These types of measures, however, do not provide much insight into why students are able to make progress toward program completion and graduation.

Approaches to the study of student success, when success is seen to include graduation, are still evolving and few in number. Some of the classic research literature on student departure, as well as some of the literature on student retention and persistence, points in the direction of student success modeling but falls short of envisioning student success as the central phenomenon of interest. To make matters more confusing, some recent studies attempt to recast the dropout literature as research on student success. In

TABLE 1.3

Taxonomy of Barriers Across Various Studies (Postsecondary Level)

Studies	Types of Barriers						
	Personal	Financial	Institutional	Learning	Coursework	Student Services	Cultural
Tinto (2002)	*	*	*				
Padilla & Pavel (1986)	*	*	*	*	*	*	
Lynch et al. (1994)		*	*		*		
Rendón (1993, 1995)	*	*	*	*		*	*
Hagedorn (2004)	*		*	*	*	*	
LeSure-Lester (2003)			*	*			
Bolge (1994a, 1994b)	*	*	*				
Kazis & Liebowitz (2003)				*			
Myhre (1998)			*		*		
Miller et al. (2005)	*	*	*	*			
Wirth (2006)	*	*	*	*	*	*	

From Wirth (2006), p. 163.

spite of this confusion, it is possible to outline the still-evolving research approaches to student success as shown in Table 1.4.

As already noted, this book focuses on the Expertise Model of Student Success. However, much more research needs to be done to explore alternate models that closely examine the process of negotiating a campus that leads students to success, including graduation.

AUTOETHNOGRAPHIC ENCOUNTER: THE TURN TO STUDENT SUCCESS

By the mid-1980s, after a five-year struggle, the Hispanic Research Center was up and running at Arizona State University. I was the newly appointed permanent director of the center. One day Alfredo de los Santos, Jr., then a vice-chancellor at the Maricopa County Community College District (MCCCD), came to my office with a disarmingly simple request. They were

TABLE 1.4
Approaches to the Study of Student Success

Approach	Exemplars	Notes
Best practices	Allen & Kazis (2007); Lumina Foundation for Education (2007); Purnell & Blank (2004); Santiago & Brown (2004); Seidman (2005); Tovar & Simon (2003); etc.	Attempt to systematize the use of institutional data and best practices to promote student success.
Correlational and descriptive studies	Gao (2002); Gerardi (1996); Kuh et al. (2005); Swail, Redd, & Perna (2003); etc.	Attempt to find relationships between various individual and environmental variables and student success.
Empirically grounded models	Hagedorn et al. (2002); Nuñez (2005); Stahl & Pavel (1992); Webb (1989); etc.	More complex correlational studies that include a conceptual model of student success.
Dynamics of success for ethnic and racial minority students	Attinasi, Jr. (1986); Berger (2000); Hurtado & Carter (1997); Lowe (1989); Rendón (1993); Rendón & Jalomo (1995); Saggio (2000); Saunders & Serna (2004); etc.	The distinctive experiences of ethnic and racial minorities are seen as important to achieving student success. Includes the concepts of student validation, cultural capital, etc.
Expertise Model of Student Success	Barker (2005); Miller (2005); Padilla (1999); Padilla & Pavel (1986); Wirth (2006); etc.	Incorporates expert systems theory to drive student success modeling based on qualitative research methods.

Citations are illustrative.

interested in promoting student success in their district, he said, and they thought that I might be able to help. Instinctively, I responded that I specialized in four-year colleges and that I didn't know very much about community college students. Alfredo was merciless. "But you are a researcher," he said. I couldn't argue with that. He also was generous. He offered money and district support. I agreed. After all, it was this kind of problem that the Hispanic Research Center was designed to address.

As I began to think about the MCCCD project, I thought about the existing knowledge base and the standard approaches then available to study such a problem. But there was something that didn't quite fit. The most popular models at that time focused on student dropouts, and Alfredo had been very clear. The district was interested in promoting "student success." I couldn't ignore that phrase and simply repackage it as a concern for dropouts. I had to find an answer to *his* problem, not the one that I could answer within existing frameworks. Struggling with the research design for the project, I finally came to an important realization, an epiphany of sorts. To put it perhaps too strongly, the field had been focusing on the wrong end of things. Most of the existing research was on dropouts, but what was really of interest was student success! Now I could see clearly why using existing frameworks was like trying to fit the proverbial square peg into a round hole. However, the afterglow of this "Eureka!" moment was short lived: I realized that there wasn't a handy extant framework on student success that I could use for the project. In fact, the more I thought about it the clearer it became that by focusing on student success I was inexorably drifting away from existing theories and methods.

As it later turned out, I was also drifting away from the community of scholars in higher education who continued to focus on dropouts rather than student success. In short, I found myself in the interesting predicament of having to propose a theoretical framework, identify the research methods that could be applied to it, and then use all this academic machinery to address the problem identified by the community college district. A tall order indeed. In fact, the order was so tall that some of my students and I have spent more than 20 years working on it. Along the way we have learned some valuable lessons about the workings of academia when it comes to shifting inquiry paradigms, as well as about studying student success. Above all, I personally have learned that the primary responsibility of a researcher is to answer the question that is being asked, not the one that is most familiar and tractable.

References

Ahrens, A. M., & Boatwright, M. A. (1997). Satisfaction with career planning and job placement services at two-year public colleges. *Community College Journal of Research and Practice, 21*(7), 617–626.

Allen, L., & Kazis, R. (2007). *Building a culture of evidence in community colleges: Lessons from exemplary institutions.* Boston: Jobs for the Future.

Astin, A. W. (1984). Student involvement: A developmental theory for higher education. *Journal of College Student Personnel, 25,* 297–308.

Attinasi, L. C., Jr. (1986). *Getting in: Chicano students' perceptions of their college-going behavior with implications for their freshman-year persistence.* Unpublished doctoral dissertation, Arizona State University.

Barker, K. S. (2005). *Overcoming barriers to high school success: Perceptions of students and those in charge of ensuring their success.* Unpublished doctoral dissertation, University of Texas at San Antonio, College of Education and Human Development.

Bean, J. P. (1983). The application of a model of turnover in work organizations to the student attrition process. *The Review of Higher Education, 6*(2), 129–148.

Bean, J. P., & Eaton, S. (2000). A psychological model of college student retention. In J. M. Braxton (Ed.), *Reworking the student departure puzzle: New theory and research on college student retention* (pp. 73–89). Nashville, TN: Vanderbilt University Press.

Berger, J. B. (2000). Optimizing capital, social reproduction, and undergraduate persistence: A sociological perspective. In J. M. Braxton (Ed.), *Reworking the student departure puzzle* (pp. 96–126). Nashville, TN: Vanderbilt University Press.

Bilsky, J. H. (2000). Student satisfaction among select demographic groups at a Florida community college. *Dissertation Abstracts International, 61,* 3035 (UMI No. 9984391)

Bolge, R. D. (1994a). *Identifying and dealing with access barriers at Mercer County Community College.* (ERIC Document Reproduction Service No. ED376876)

Bolge, R. D. (1994b). *Examination of the learning and psycho-social skills needed by and barriers for remedial students at Mercer Community College.* (ERIC Document Reproduction Service No. ED382240)

Borglum, K. M. (1998). Stop, drop, enroll: An analysis of student satisfaction, and withdrawal from a metropolitan community college. *Dissertation Abstracts International, 59,* 2317 (UMI No. 9841686)

Bourdon, C. M., & Carducci, R. (2002). *What works in the community colleges: A synthesis of the literature on best practices.* (ERIC Document Reproduction Service No. ED471397)

Braxton, J. M. (2003). Student success. In S. R. Komives & D. B. Woodard, Jr. (Eds.), *Student services: A handbook for the profession* (4th ed., pp. 317–338). San Francisco: Jossey-Bass.

CCSSE. (2004). *Engagement by design: Findings 2004.* Austin: The University of Texas at Austin, Community College Leadership Program.

CCSSE. (2005). *Engaging students, challenging the odds.* Austin: The University of Texas at Austin, Community College Leadership Program.

CCSSE. (2007). *Committing to student engagement; Reflections on CCSSE's first five years.* Austin: The University of Texas at Austin, Community College Leadership Program.

Chickering, A. W., & Gamson, Z. F. (1987). Seven principles for good practice in undergraduate education. *American Association for Higher Education (AAHE) Bulletin, 39*(7), 3–7.

Cofer, J., & Somers, P. (2000). Within-year persistence of students at two-year colleges. *Community College Journal of Research and Practice, 24*(10), 785–807.

Dörner, D. (1989). *The logic of failure: Recognizing and avoiding error in complex situations.* New York: Perseus.

Dweck, C. S. (2000). *Self-theories: Their role in motivation, personality, and development.* Philadelphia: Psychology Press.

Fallows, R. (1987). *A study of persistence of American Indian students at a large Southwestern university.* Unpublished doctoral dissertation, Arizona State University.

Friedlander, J., Pace, C. R., Murrell, P., & Lehman, P. W. (1990, revised 1999). *The Community College Student Experience Questionnaire.* Memphis, TN: University of Memphis, Center for the Study Higher Education.

Gao, H. (2002). *Examining the length of time to completion at a community college.* (ERIC Document Reproduction Service No. ED475987)

Garza, E., Reyes, P., & Trueba, E. T. (2004). *Resiliency and success: Migrant children in the U.S.* Boulder, CO: Paradigm.

Gerardi, S. (1996). *Factors which influence community college graduation.* (ERIC Document Reproduction Service No. ED398945)

Goldin, C., Katz, L. F., & Kuziemko, I. (2006, March). *The homecoming of American college women: The reversal of the college gender gap* (NBER Working Paper 12139). Cambridge, MAQ: National Bureau of Economic Research.

Gordon, K. (1996). Resilient Hispanic youths' self-concept and motivational patterns. *Hispanic Journal of Behavioral Science, 18*(1), 63–73.

Hagedorn, L. S. (2004). *The role of the urban community college in educating diverse populations.* New Directions for Community Colleges, Number 127. San Francisco: Jossey-Bass.

Hagedorn, L. S., Moon, H. S., Maxwell, W., & Pickett, M. C. (2002). *Community college model of student life and retention.* Retrieved April 30, 2005, from http://www .usc.edu/dept/education/truccs/Papers/Interplay_QSL_CC-AERAfinal3.pdf

Hilliard, A. (2003). *Young, gifted and Black: Promoting high achievement among African-American students.* Boston: Beacon Press.

Hurtado, S., & Carter, D. F. (1997). Effects of college transition and perceptions of the campus racial climate on Latino students' sense of belonging. *Sociology of Education, 70*(4), 324–345.

Kazis, R., & Liebowitz, M. (2003). *Opening doors to earning credentials: Curricular and program format innovations that help low-income students succeed in community colleges.* (ERIC Document Reproduction Service No. ED475990)

Kuh, G. D. (1999). A framework for understanding student affairs work. *Journal of College Student Development, 40*(5), 530–537.

Kuh, G. D., Kinzie, J., Buckley, J. A., Bridges, B. K., & Hayek, J. C. (2006). *What matters to student success: A review of the literature.* Commissioned report for the National Symposium on Postsecondary Student Success: Spearheading a Dialog on Student Success. Washington, DC: National Postsecondary Education Cooperative.

Kuh, G. D., Kinzie, J., Schuh, J. H., & Whitt, E. J. (2005). *Student success in college: Creating conditions that matter.* San Francisco: Jossey-Bass.

Kuh, G. D., & Love, P.G. (2000). A cultural perspective on student departure. In J. M. Braxton (Ed.), *Reworking the student departure puzzle* (pp. 196–212). Nashville, TN: Vanderbilt University Press.

Kuh, G., Pace, C., & Vesper, N. (1997). The development of process indicators to estimate student gains associated with good practices in undergraduate education. *Research in Higher Education, 38*(4), 435–454.

LeSure-Lester, G. E. (2003). Effects of coping styles on college persistence decisions among Latino students in two-year colleges. *Journal of College Student Retention, 5*(11), 11–22.

Lowe, M. (1989). *Chicano students' perceptions of their community college experience, with implications for persistence: A naturalistic inquiry.* Unpublished doctoral dissertation, Arizona State University.

Lumina Foundation for Education. (2007). *Places—and faces—that foster student success.* Indianapolis, IN: Author.

Lynch, R., Harnish, D., & Brown, T. G. (1994). *Seamless education: Barriers to transfer in postsecondary education.* (ERIC Document Reproduction Service No. ED391103)

McMillan, J. H., & Reed, D. F. (1994). At risk students and resiliency: Factors contributing to academic success. *Clearing House, 67*(3), 137–140.

Melchior-Walsh, S. (1994). *Sociocultural alienation: Experiences of North American Indian students in higher education.* Unpublished doctoral dissertation, Arizona State University.

Miller, M. (2005). *Accounting for student and school success in high poverty, high minority schools: A constructivist approach.* Unpublished doctoral dissertation, University of Texas at San Antonio.

Miller, M. T., Pope, M. L., & Steinmann, T. D. (2005). Dealing with the challenges and stressors faced by community college students: The old try. *Community College Journal of Research and Practice, 29*(1), *63–7.*

Myhre, J. R. (1998). *Traveling the transfer path: Student experiences at City College of San Francisco* (ERIC Document Reproduction Service No. ED416946).

National Center for Education Statistics. (2004). *The condition of education 2004.* Washington, DC: U.S. Department of Education, Institute of Education Sciences. (NCES 2004–077)

National Center for Education Statistics. (2006). Digest of education statistics. Retrieved August 27, 2007, from http://nces.ed.gov/pubsearch/pubsinfo.asp?pubid=2004077

Nora, A. (2004). The role of habitus and cultural capital in choosing a college, transitioning from high school to higher education, and persisting in college among minority and nonminority students. *Journal of Hispanic Higher Education, 3*(2), 180–208.

Nuñez, A. M. (2005). *Modeling college transitions of Latino students.* Unpublished doctoral dissertation, University of California at Los Angeles. (UMI No. 3190475)

Pace, C. R. (1984). *Measuring the quality of college student experiences.* Los Angeles, CA: University of California at Los Angeles, Higher Education Research Institute.

Padilla, R. V. (1999). College student retention: Focus on success. *Journal of College Student Retention: Research, Theory & Practice, 1*(2), 131–145.

Padilla, R. V., & Pavel, M. (1986). *Successful Hispanic community college students: An exploratory qualitative study.* Tempe: Arizona State University, Hispanic Research Center.

Purnell, R., & Blank, S. (2004). *Support success. Services that may help low-income students succeed in community college.* Retrieved May 5, 2005, from http://www.mdrc.org/publications/399/full.pdf

Rendón, L. I. (1993). Validating culturally diverse students: Toward a new model of learning and student development. (ERIC Document Reproduction Service No. ED371672)

Rendón, L. I. (1995). Facilitating retention and transfer for first generation students in community colleges. (ERIC Document Reproduction Service No. ED383369)

Rendón, L. I., & Jalomo, R. E. (1995). Validating student experience and promoting progress, performance, and persistence through assessment. (ERIC Document Reproduction Service No. ED381051)

Rendón, L. I., Jalomo, R. E., & Nora, A. (2000). Theoretical considerations in the study of minority student retention in higher education. In J. Braxton (Ed.), *Reworking the student departure puzzle: New theory and research on college student retention* (pp. 127–156). Nashville, TN: Vanderbilt University Press.

Rousseau, D. M. (1995). *Psychological contract in organizations: Understanding written and unwritten agreements.* Newbury Park, CA: Sage.

Rowland, S. L. (2003). Factors that contribute to the persistence and academic achievement of community college students. *Dissertation Abstracts International, 64,* 425. (UMI No. 3081447)

Saggio, J. J. (2000). *Experiences affecting post freshman retention of American Indian/ Alaskan Native students at a Bible college.* Unpublished doctoral dissertation, Arizona State University.

Santiago, D. A., & Brown, S. E. (2004). *What works for Latino students.* Washington, DC: *Excelencia* in Education.

Saunders, M., & Serna, I. (2004). Making college happen: The college experiences of first-generation Latino students. *Journal of Hispanic Higher Education, 3*(2), 246–163.

Seidman, A. (2005). Formula for student success. In A. Seidman (Ed.), *College student retention: Formula for success* (pp. 132–145). Westport, CT: Praeger.

Stahl, V. V., & Pavel, D. M. (1992). *Assessing the Bean and Metzner model with community college student data.* (ERIC Document Reproduction Service No. ED344639)

Stehr, N. (1992). *Practical knowledge: Applying the social sciences.* Newbury Park, CA: Sage.

St. John, E. P., Cabrerra, A. F., Nora, A., & Asker, E. H. (2000). Economic influences on persistence reconsidered: How can finance research inform the reconceptualiztion of persistence models? In J. M. Braxton (Ed.), *Reworking the student departure puzzle* (pp. 29–47). Nashville, TN: Vanderbilt University Press.

Swail, W. S., Redd, K. E., & Perna, L. W. (2003). Retaining minority students in higher education: A framework for success. In A. J. Kezar (Series Ed.), *ASHE-ERIC Higher Education Report: Volume 30, Number 2.* Hoboken, NJ: Wiley.

Tierney, W. G. (1993). *Building communities of difference: Higher education in the twenty-first century.* Westport, CT: Bergin & Garvey.

Tinto, V. (1987). *Leaving college: Rethinking the causes and cures of student attrition.* Chicago: University of Chicago Press.

Tinto, V. (2000). Linking learning and leaving: Exploring the role of the college classroom in student departure. In J. M. Braxton (Ed.), *Reworking the student departure puzzle* (pp. 81–94). Nashville, TN: Vanderbilt University Press.

Tinto, V. (2002, June). *Promoting student retention: Lessons learned from the United States.* Paper presented at the 11th Annual Conference of the European Access Network, Prato, Italy.

Tovar, E., & Simon, M. A. (2003). *Facilitating student success for entering California community college students: How one institution can make an impact.* (ERIC Document Reproduction Service No. ED476679)

Webb, M. (1989). A theoretical model of community college student persistence. *Community College Review, 16*(4), 42–49.

White, R. (2004). Predicting the persistence of information technology students. *Dissertation Abstracts International, 65,* 2900 (UMI No. 3141905).

Wirth, R. M. (2006). Student and advisor perspectives on student success in a community college in south Texas. Unpublished doctoral dissertation, University of Texas at San Antonio.

2

SEARCHING FOR
THEORY AND METHOD

The Expertise Model of Student Success (EMSS) is based on a set of assumptions about how students experience the campus and on conceptual borrowings from expert systems theory. It also relies on qualitative research methods to gather data through what can be called a "qualitative survey." Data analysis is accomplished through the development of taxonomies and "concept modeling." The end product is a local student success model (LSSM) for the subject campus that can be used to help promote student success. This chapter provides the details for these aspects of EMSS.

Assumptions of EMSS

There are four assumptions underlying EMSS. The first assumption is simply an acknowledgment that, at the end of the day, we have not yet been able to explain why one student can enter a campus, begin studies, and eventually graduate, while another student entering campus at the same time can fail to follow a program of studies to graduation. Given this lack of understanding, we can take a lesson from our colleagues in the physical sciences and simply treat the campus experience as a "black box": We know what goes into the black box and also what comes out of it, but not much about what happens inside. In other words, we know quite a bit about the students when they begin their studies—previous grades, subjects studied, test results, etc.—and also about the students when they graduate. However, we don't know much about what accounts for one student succeeding (making progress and graduating) while another student drops out before completing a program of study (see Figure 2.1).

FIGURE 2.1
Assumption of the Campus Experience as a "Black Box"

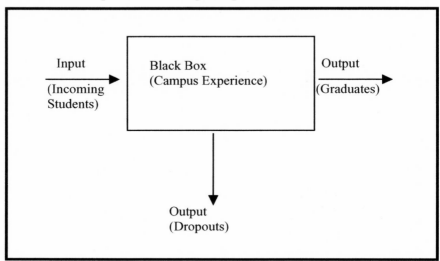

At first blush this assumption might seem to quash all hope of understanding student success. However, our colleagues in the physical sciences are not so easily deterred when facing a similar situation. Not knowing how an atom is put together, physical scientists simply resorted to smashing the atom with high-velocity particles to see what would come out. They took the atom to be a "black box" that can be explored profitably by examining carefully the inputs and the outputs. Of course, students generally should not be smashed, but we can find other ways of probing their experiences if we first make the next assumption.

The second assumption holds that from a student's perspective the campus in which the student is enrolled presents a series of barriers to his or her academic progress and graduation. In the 1980s, Louis Attinasi (1986) conducted a dissertation study in which he investigated the "getting in" of Chicano students who enrolled in a large Southwestern public university. Since many of these students came from rural areas and small towns and the university had a very large student population and was located in a large metropolitan area, many of these students found it necessary to cope with barriers of scale after they arrived on campus. Attinasi identified three such barriers. One barrier related to the physical size of the campus. The campus was just too large for these students. In order to survive, the students had to scale down the campus geography so that they could deal with only a part of the campus, the part that was most relevant to their studies. The rest of the campus largely could be ignored.

Generalizing the concept of physical geography, Attinasi identified two other geographies that also needed to be scaled down by the students: the social and academic aspects of the university. The social aspects of the university were challenging for the students because there was no way that they could interact effectively with the thousands of students on campus. Compared to their small communities of origin where "everybody knew everybody," the large university campus provided many more opportunities for contact with other students of diverse backgrounds. The students solved this problem by scaling down the social environment on campus. They interacted primarily with a relevant subset of students and mostly ignored the rest. They treated the campus academic geography in the same manner. The number of courses, majors, careers, etc., on a large university campus is simply overwhelming, so the students scaled down the campus academic geography by selecting a major and focusing mostly on the coursework needed to graduate from the department offering the major. Interestingly, selecting a major also provided the students with a means to scale down the social geography of the campus, because academic departments often are centers for social activity.

A general point from Attinasi's work is that students face barriers to success when they arrive on campus to pursue their studies. Restating this point in terms of the first assumption, we can assume that the campus experience (i.e., the black box) is actually the experience of a geography of barriers that each student must resolve while in the black box (see Figure 2.2).

For the students that Attinasi studied, scale was a significant aspect of the barriers that they faced. But other students from different backgrounds would not necessarily face the same types of barriers. However, they would face barriers related to their background and prior experiences in the context of the campus in which they enrolled. In short, all students face barriers: some more, some less. Not all students face the exact same set of barriers or with the same degree of severity. But all students face some set of barriers to their progress and graduation. It is these campus barriers that students must overcome if they are to make academic progress and graduate.

FIGURE 2.2
Assumption of the Campus as a Geography of Barriers Facing Students

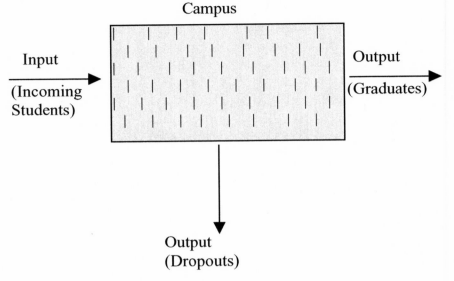

The third assumption of EMSS accounts for the ability of some students to overcome the barriers to success. The assumption is that students who are successful are students who are experts at being students. They use their expertise to overcome the barriers to success that confront them and also to meet the academic knowledge requirements for graduation. The work of Harmon and King (1985) on expert systems can be modified and used to understand what expertise means in the context of being a student (see Figure 2.3).

Student expertise consists of the total knowledge possessed by the student at graduation (i.e., compiled knowledge). Compiled knowledge has two components: heuristic (informal) and academic (formal) knowledge. Academic knowledge is campus-independent and includes laws, axioms, principles, facts, and theories. It is typically acquired in the classroom, library, or laboratory through readings, lectures, demonstrations, exercises, etc. For graduation purposes, academic knowledge is packaged as courses, and the content of and time spent on such courses leads to academic credits that are applied toward graduation. Examinations and grades are the typical indicators of student success in mastering academic knowledge. When enough course credits are accrued at the proper grade-point average over a specified range of courses, the student is allowed to graduate with a diploma or degree.

FIGURE 2.3
The Nature of Student Expertise

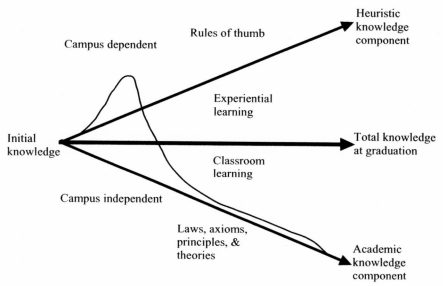

(After Harmon & King, 1985)

In contrast, heuristic knowledge is campus dependent and is mostly acquired informally by the student as the student experiences the campus. Heuristic knowledge consists of rules of thumb and situated knowledge that are spread by word of mouth and through contact with faculty, staff, and other students, and that are garnered from family members and friends who have already gone to college and through serendipitous encounters. Except for the customary freshman orientation session and the often convoluted information contained in official catalogues, students generally are on their own when it comes to acquiring heuristic knowledge. Yet overcoming many of the barriers they face throughout their career as students depends on accurate heuristic knowledge. Even the acquisition of academic knowledge can depend on heuristic knowledge in terms of knowing how to get tutoring, which courses to take and their sequence, major selection, exam-taking skills, etc. Heuristic knowledge, therefore, is central to student success.

As shown in Figure 2.3, students arrive on campus with preexisting compiled knowledge based on their prior experiences and schooling. As they engage in further academic study, they must increase their academic knowledge sufficiently to meet the graduation requirements for their program of study. At the same time, all students must acquire sufficient heuristic knowledge to allow them to overcome the barriers to their success. The curve in the figure shows the hypothesized distribution of academic and heuristic knowledge as suggested in a different study by Harmon and King (1985).

Heuristic knowledge must be acquired in large volume early in the program of study. As the student progresses toward graduation, the amount of heuristic knowledge needed tapers off while the amount of academic knowledge continues to increase. In practical terms, this means that, once a student has figured out "the system," only incremental amounts of heuristic knowledge are needed for continued success. This hypothesized distribution of heuristic and academic knowledge is consistent with past research, which shows that the majority of dropouts in high school and college occur during the freshman year. EMSS accounts for this finding by suggesting that the lack of heuristic knowledge early on can lead to early dropping out.

Because the teaching and learning of academic knowledge has been studied for many years, while the study of heuristic knowledge has been mostly neglected, the Expertise Model of Student Success concentrates on the role and identification of heuristic knowledge in modeling student success. However, the important role of academic knowledge should not be underestimated. It is important to remember that compiled knowledge (expertise) entails both heuristic and academic knowledge, and that both are needed in sufficient quantities if the student is to be successful.

The fourth assumption involves conation. Conation refers to action or the will to act. Heuristic knowledge is necessary but not sufficient to overcome barriers to success. To overcome such barriers the student also must take effective actions. The set of effective actions determines a student's behavioral repertoire for success. So in order to model student success we must identify both the heuristic knowledge base and the action repertoire of successful students. Combining all of the assumptions, it can be seen that EMSS includes three parameters: namely the barriers to success plus the knowledge and the actions that successful students use to overcome the barriers.

EMSS can be summarized (see Figure 2.4) as a *general model of student success* (GMSS). Students enter a program of study (campus) that will require them to master in a specified manner a body of academic knowledge and skills. To achieve this task, students will need to complete a series of courses and examinations at a specified performance level. When their program of

FIGURE 2.4
EMSS as a General Model of Student Success

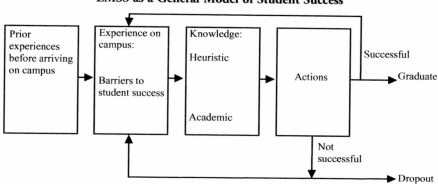

study is completed, students will be rewarded with a diploma or degree and graduation. Students at the postsecondary level normally must pay tuition and fees, and all students must possess enough resources to subsist while they are studying. Besides studying, students often also have to meet various responsibilities involving family, employers, significant others, etc. In addition, students may be experiencing life-course developmental changes that demand their energy and attention.

As a result of these and other factors, students face any number of barriers to their success. To overcome these barriers, students must know about effective solutions and then actually implement them. If students are able to amass the required heuristic knowledge and indeed take effective actions, they will be able to overcome or avoid the barriers and, if they also have acquired the required academic knowledge, eventually graduate. Students arrive on campus with preexisting levels of academic and heuristic knowledge, as well as action strategies, that have worked in the past. However, there is no guarantee that the prior knowledge and actions will be relevant or effective in the new campus environment. So from the start students face the challenge of acquiring new academic and heuristic knowledge so that they can meet academic knowledge requirements and generate the know-how to overcome barriers as they are encountered.

The Local Student Success Model

EMSS as a general student success model specifies three parameters: the barriers that students encounter, the knowledge they use to identify effective solutions, and the actions they take to actually overcome the barriers. These three parameters can be determined for any given campus and any desired student population ranging from the campus as a whole to identifiable subpopulations. The empirical determination of these parameters creates an instance of the EMSS that is designated as the local student success model. LSSMs, therefore, are campus specific. They speak to the nature of the black box experience on a given campus and how it is that some students on that campus can be successful in completing their program of study to graduate. Because of its local nature, the LSSM can be used to drive local institutional strategies to improve student success. This is a feature of student success modeling that generally has been absent in other models.

So the data requirements for creating an LSSM are simple and straightforward: Identify the campus barriers to success for a given student population; identify the heuristic knowledge that these students possess to overcome the barriers; and identify the actions that these students take to overcome the barriers. Clearly, meeting these data demands could be achieved using various strategies. The qualitative strategy currently used in EMSS is described below.

Methods and Procedures

In principle it should be possible to gather the required data using either qualitative or quantitative approaches. To date, the preferred approach has been qualitative. Since it is assumed that students are the experts at being students, the students are an important source of data. However, other sources of data also are important, including faculty, staff, and administrators. At some educational levels, parents and family members also may be important data sources. Still other sources of data include previous studies, catalogues, databases, documents, and observations that pertain to the campus. The latter are especially important for developing the concept model of student success.

Identifying the barriers, knowledge, and actions amounts to capturing the knowledge base possessed by successful students (experts) at a particular campus. Although this task could be accomplished by doing individual interviews with students, it is more efficiently accomplished using group interviews. One of the advantages of interviewing small groups is that interviewees tend to self-correct as information is provided by other individuals. Through dialogue with each other or with the session moderator, the interviewees have an opportunity to clarify what they mean. Group interviews thus have a built-in cross-check on the quality of the data being gathered.

The main instrument used to capture the qualitative data is the "unfolding matrix" (Padilla, 1994; see Figure 2.5). The matrix consists of three columns: one column each for barriers, knowledge, and actions. As many rows are added to the matrix as there are barriers identified by the interviewees.

Following the work of Spradley (1979), the words at the top of each column are designated "cover terms." Any cover term can be "unfolded," or expanded semantically, by providing examples of the various meanings that the cover term may encompass. Each distinct meaning, called an exemplar, is captured in one of the cells in the rows beneath the cover term. The task of the interviewees is to complete the matrix by providing, as exhaustively as possible, the exemplars for each of the cover terms.

For example, in the case of the cover term "barriers," the interviewees will identify all the barriers that successful students encounter and resolve while engaged in a program of study on campus. As interviewees identify the barriers, each barrier is entered in a separate row below the cover term "barriers." After interviewees have exhaustively identified the barriers to success, they will identify the knowledge that successful students possess that allows them to overcome each barrier. This information is entered under the cover

FIGURE 2.5
The Unfolding Matrix with Three Columns and an Indefinite Number of Rows

Barriers	Knowledge	Actions

term "knowledge" in the row corresponding to the barrier in question. All the knowledge exemplars for a given barrier are entered in one cell.

When the interviewees have provided all the exemplars of the knowledge cover term, they turn their attention to the "actions" cover term. At this point the interviewees provide exemplars of actions that successful students take to overcome each barrier. The action exemplars are entered into the matrix in the cell underneath the "actions" cover term that corresponds to the barrier in question. When the matrix is completed, the investigator will have acquired the set of barriers, the body of knowledge used to overcome them, and the actions that are taken to overcome the barriers for the subject campus. Clearly, if the students are the data source for completing the matrix, the exemplars will represent a student perspective. If it is desirable to do so, the investigator also may complete a matrix with other participants on campus, such as faculty, professional staff, or administrators. Although this expanded data collection entails use of greater resources, the enhanced data will provide multiple perspectives on student success and may help to pinpoint different sets of problems on campus.

Typically, the physical matrix is constructed using rolled paper ("butcher paper") that is cut into appropriate lengths to accommodate the number of columns needed. The cells need to be large enough so that an assistant (the scribe) can enter the data in each cell with a felt pen. The writing needs to be large enough so that the interviewees can read what is in each cell from wherever they are sitting. The strips of paper are taped to a smooth wall at a convenient height. The cells can be created with a straight edge, with the cover terms clearly printed at the top of each column. To keep track of the order of the lengths of paper, each one should be numbered, so that the matrix can be reassembled in the correct order after it is taken down from the wall. It also is a good idea to date the matrix and identify the campus where it was completed.

It is good practice to audio record the group interviews. The audio recording will provide a backup for the data as well as a resource for clarifying the meaning of an exemplar if, when the exemplar later is read from the matrix, its meaning has become cryptic. Audio recording will require written permission from the interviewees and may become a distraction. To minimize the latter, the moderator should assure the students that all information given by them will be kept confidential and that they will not be identified as individuals. For this reason, it is important that the interviewees not introduce themselves by name during the session. As a welcoming gesture, the moderator should introduce them as a group. Although the group interview also could be video recorded, the investigator must weigh carefully the advantages of any additional data that may be gained against the enhanced disruptive potential and the threat to confidentiality that video recording might pose.

Selecting students for participation in the group interviews needs to be done with care. Students do not have to be randomly selected, but it is important to select students who represent the diversity of students present on campus. Note that the interviewees are not necessarily a sample of successful or outstanding students. All students potentially have knowledge about the barriers and the knowledge and actions needed to overcome them. What is important is that students have sufficient experience on campus to be able to provide accurate and comprehensive exemplars for the matrix. At the high school and four-year-college levels, students with junior or senior standing generally are the indicated subjects. At the two-year-college level, students with at least one or two semesters on campus should be recruited as participants.

The mix of students recruited depends on the focus of the inquiry, or, more technically, the unit of analysis. If the focus is on the campus as a whole, then the sample should be drawn to represent this level of analysis. If the focus is on a particular racial, ethnic, or gender group, then the sample should be drawn consistent with the characteristics of the selected group. It is the same for other identity or demographic groups, such as international students, older students, residential students, commuter students, and part-time students. Through the study of subpopulations the set of barriers, along with the knowledge and actions used to overcome these barriers, can be identified for particular groups of students who may have special needs. Thus, a campus can target its services so that general problems have general solutions and special problems have special solutions. This will help to avoid unnecessary redundancies in student services provided, while ensuring that the needs of all students are being met.

The group interviews—sometimes referred to as focus groups or dialogical interviews—consist of small groups of participants, usually 5 to 10 subjects. If the group is too small the participants may feel inhibited or too exposed. If it is too large there will not be enough time or opportunity for all participants to share their knowledge. Since no-shows can be expected, it is wise to recruit 10 to 12 students, expecting that several may not show up for the actual interview. To minimize no-shows, it may be helpful to remind the students through a phone call or email. Providing small rewards or incentives also may help. These can include refreshments, snacks, raffles, or small stipends. Snacks such as pizza are especially effective if the interview is conducted near or during a meal time.

The duration of a group interview can be adjusted to meet local conditions, but it generally should last 50 minutes to an hour. Participation in this type of interview can be quite exhausting for the subjects, so longer times can lead to diminished productivity. As a strategy to overcome the loss of energy, tandem group interviews can be conducted.

Previous experience has shown that at least three tandem group interviews are needed to complete one matrix. The first group is interviewed for the designated time and completes as much of the matrix as it can. The first group always starts with the barriers and continues with the matrix until its time is exhausted. Immediately after the first group, the second group continues with matrix completion until its time is exhausted. The second group is given the opportunity to briefly go over the work of the previous group and also to add barriers if they can think of any. It is important not to dwell too long on this introductory review. When the time allotted to the second group is exhausted, the third group takes over. This group also is given a moment to review the previous work and to add any new barriers. The group then continues to complete the matrix. If there are gaps in the matrix after the third group session has concluded, the investigator should seriously consider assembling a fourth group to make sure that the matrix has no empty cells.

The amount and quality of the data gathered depends on the skills of the interview session moderator. This individual must be skilled in eliciting participant responses, especially when an interviewee is struggling to communicate some idea or bit of information. The moderator should help the individual to articulate what he or she is trying to say without substituting the moderator's own words or ideas for those of the interviewee. Sometimes this can be accomplished by inviting group participation. However, if the group gets bogged down with extended discussions, it may become unproductive in completing the matrix. It is up to the moderator to keep the group productive while making sure that the subjects' perspectives are being captured in the matrix.

Moderator skills can be enhanced through training and by doing a pilot session with a few participants before the actual data collection. The pilot session also will provide an opportunity to practice the logistics of running tandem group interviews, including the training of the scribe, manipulation of the recording equipment, signing of paperwork, providing refreshments and snacks, making the physical matrix, finding a room for the interview, etc.

The data analysis is likely to be more fruitful if the analyst moderates the group interviews or at least is present while someone else is moderating. Since moderating a session is very demanding and exhausting, it is wise not to attempt to moderate more than one session in quick succession. The moderator should keep an eye on the matrix at all times while it is being completed. As a general rule, the moderator should determine what the scribe writes in each cell. If the scribe interprets what is being said by the interviewees and writes it down in the cells, the moderator later may not know the meaning of what was written down, or worse, the scribe's perspective may be captured at the expense of the participant perspectives.

The quality of the data is enhanced if the moderator carefully primes the participants. Interviewees will want to know what is expected of them. After the preliminaries are completed—including welcoming and assuring confidentiality—the following primer can be used with the first group:

> *Think of a successful student on this campus, one who is making progress toward graduation and whom the student and others expect will graduate. What are some barriers that such a successful student must overcome in order to be successful?*

Give the interviewees a moment or two to think about this. Answer any questions that may arise. As soon as someone volunteers a barrier, record it (clarify if necessary) on the matrix and solicit other barriers. Whenever there is extended silence, repeat the primer and encourage the students to keep identifying additional barriers. It is important not to rush the interviewees or to close the identification of exemplars prematurely.

After the barriers have been identified, the interviewees can be primed for the knowledge exemplars. A primer such as the following can be used:

> *You have done a good job in identifying the barriers that successful students*
> *face and overcome on this campus. Now let's think about what such students*
> *know about each barrier that allows them to overcome it.*

Give the participants a moment or two to think. Then, starting with the first barrier from the top, ask the participants to give exemplars of what successful students know that allows them to overcome the barrier. It is important to distinguish between what successful students *know* and what they *do* to overcome a barrier. If a participant contributes an action as a knowledge exemplar, gently remind the group that you will be asking for actions shortly and that at this point you want to focus on what students know (see discussion of actions below). If knowledge and actions become commingled at this point, it will be very difficult to distinguish between knowledge and actions during the analysis. If the second group works on the knowledge exemplars, they can be primed in a similar manner, first with the meaning of a successful student and then for knowledge exemplars.

After all the knowledge exemplars have been entered into the matrix the interviewees can be primed for action exemplars:

> *Good job in identifying the knowledge possessed by successful students. Let's go*
> *back to the top and, for each barrier, think about the actions that successful*
> *students on this campus take to overcome the barrier. We have identified what*
> *successful students know; now let's identify what they actually do.*

Identify the first barrier to focus attention, briefly summarize what successful students *know* about this barrier, and invite the participants to identify what successful students *do*. There can be a close connection between knowledge and actions. For example, if a knowledge exemplar is "know to file financial aid application before the deadline," the action might simply be "file the financial aid application before the deadline." Of course, some actions are not as tightly coupled to the knowledge exemplars. However, even for those action exemplars that are tightly coupled with the knowledge exemplars, it is important for the participants to articulate the actions and not assume them.

Notice that this example also provides a strategy for handling actions that are offered during the knowledge collection stage. If a student offers "file the financial aid application before the deadline," the moderator can respond, "We are focusing on knowledge at this point; do you mean that the successful student 'knows to file the financial aid application before the deadline'?" This can save the day and alert the participants about expressing knowledge as opposed to action exemplars.

Although the unfolding matrix with only three columns of data is adequate for developing the LSSM, it may be desirable to add two more columns as a way to obtain a richer data set (see Figure 2.6). Since the barriers to success have been identified, it is useful to ask the interviewees to identify changes that the institution could make to diminish or eliminate each of the barriers. So the cover term for the fourth column would be "changes."

In addition, if the suggested changes actually were made, problems, including unintended consequences, might result for the institution, the students, or others. By adding a fifth column to the matrix, participants can identify what they think would be the most likely problems to occur from making the suggested changes. Therefore, the cover term for the fifth column is "problems." Starting with the first barrier, the participants are asked to think about and identify any changes by the institution that would lessen or eliminate that barrier. After the changes are identified for a given barrier, participants are asked to identify likely problems that would occur if the changes were implemented. In other words, both changes and problems are identified for each barrier before proceeding to the next one. These additional cover terms can be quite useful in providing suggestions for reducing or eliminating barriers on campus and thus enhancing student success.

The completed matrix becomes an important data set for later analysis. It is best to clarify any cell entries that are not clear while the participants

FIGURE 2.6
The Expanded Unfolding Matrix with Two Additional Cover Terms

Barriers	Knowledge	Actions	Changes	Problems

are still assembled. If there are any empty cells, it may be necessary to assemble another group interview to make sure that the data set is complete.

Data Analysis

The local student success model can be expressed simply as a taxonomy of the various cover terms contained in the unfolding matrix. In other words, this type of LSSM results from data reduction through taxonomic analysis of the qualitative data in the matrix. A more elaborate LSSM can be constructed through concept modeling, in which data synthesis is accomplished through the inductive formation of concepts based on both the data from the unfolding matrix and other data gathered from the campus. Thus, the taxonomic LSSM is reductive, while the LSSM as concept model has both a reductive aspect, as concepts are identified, and a synthetic aspect, when the concepts are integrated through a set of relationships that bind them into a meaningful whole. For now the analytic focus will be on the taxonomic LSSM. The LSSM as a concept model will be discussed subsequently.

A taxonomy is simply a set of categories or classes. A category or class also can be thought of as a concept. So in EMSS the terms *category*, *class*, and *concept* are used almost interchangeably. This may not seem so unreasonable when we consider that these terms refer to specifying a difference among what otherwise would be undifferentiated meanings or things. If a difference in question is designated as "delta," then a taxonomy can be seen as a collection of deltas that is used to reduce some population of semantic elements or things into a distinct set of categories of meaning based on the deltas. The identification of a particular delta is done inductively and interpretively as the analyst becomes immersed in the data. Clearly, then, this type of analysis is interpretive, which is consistent with the qualitative nature of the data collected.

Because of the manner in which data are collected in the unfolding matrix, it turns out that taxonomies based on the unfolding matrix can be constructed either contingently or noncontingently. The taxonomy for the barriers cover term is always noncontingent. However, the taxonomies for the knowledge and action cover terms can be either contingent or noncontingent.

A noncontingent taxonomy is created when the categories of the taxonomy have no constraints placed on them (other than the deltas). A contingent taxonomy is constrained in the sense that the population of elements (exemplars) to be taxonomized itself belongs to a category from a preexisting taxonomy. Typically, the barriers cover term is taxonomized first. It is done so noncontingently. However, when it comes to taxonomizing the knowledge cover term, one can choose either to classify only those elements (exemplars) that pertain to a particular category of barriers (contingent analysis) or simply to ignore the barrier categories and taxonomize all of the knowledge exemplars as a whole across all barriers (noncontingently). Clearly, a contingent analysis of the knowledge exemplars will result in as many taxonomies as there are categories of barriers, while there will be only one taxonomy resulting from the noncontingent analysis of knowledge exemplars.

The taxonomies can be presented either graphically or in tabular form. Figure 2.7 shows a graphic representation of a noncontingent taxonomy of barriers for a large, urban campus in the Southwest. The subjects were Hispanic and Native American undergraduates. Originally there were more than 20 barriers identified by these students. Those barriers have been reduced to four categories through the use of four deltas, namely "discontinuity," "lack of nurturing," "lack of presence," and "resources." If desired, the actual barriers corresponding to each category could be included in the graphic to show more detail. Notice that in further theorizing the data the barriers now can be referenced through the barrier categories rather than by naming each barrier individually. In other words, data reduction can be a useful tool to aid in theorizing data.

The taxonomy in Figure 2.7 helps to explain the black box campus experience of the subject students. One category of barriers relates to the discontinuities that can occur for students as they transition from high school to college or from work to college. In addition, the subject minority students also felt that they were not nurtured on campus, as shown by the second category of barriers. This lack of nurturing was intensified by the lack of presence that these students felt as they engaged instructors and courses that did not reflect their own ethnic background and experiences. Finally, these students also experienced resource barriers, including problems with financial aid, the need to get a part-time job, etc. As can be seen, the taxonomic LSSM can be useful as a means to elaborate and theorize the data.

As already noted, a taxonomic LSSM can be displayed in tabular form also. Table 2.1 provides an example of such a display. This taxonomy was derived from barriers provided by White non-Hispanic undergraduate students at a public university in south Texas where the predominant population in the community is Hispanic. For this group, the predominant barriers

FIGURE 2.7
Example of a Noncontingent Taxonomy of Barriers Displayed Graphically

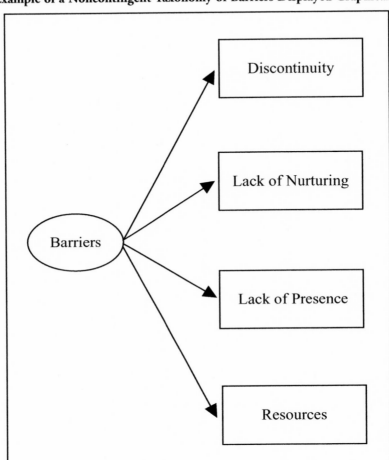

can be categorized as academic, personal, informational, financial, or related to the physical aspects of the campus. When multiple data matrices are completed by various subpopulations on a given campus, the resulting taxonomies of barriers can be compared to determine possible differences in how those subpopulations are experiencing the campus. Additional examples of contingent and noncontingent taxonomies are shown in later chapters.

When the LSSM is presented as a concept model (see Figure 2.8) it can include the taxonomic LSSM, but the concept model typically goes beyond

TABLE 2.1

Example of a Taxonomy of Barriers for Data Obtained from White Non-Hispanic Undergraduates in a Public University in South Texas

Category of Barriers	Exemplars (Barriers)
Academic	• Unrealistic student expectations about degree programs • Lack of information about degree programs • Class scheduling • Lack of information about 2 + 2 programs • Faculty spread too thin • Availability of Internet classes • Access to facilities • Lack of tutoring/TA for upper-division classes • Closing classes that are needed • Access to faculty/advisors • Classes too large • Availability of classes • Advising • Communication
Personal	• Unrealistic student expectations about degree programs • Class scheduling • Jobs • Partying/drugs
Information	• Communication • Unrealistic student expectations about degree programs • Lack of information about degree programs • Lack of information about 2 + 2 programs • Communication between students and administration • Access to faculty/advisors
Financial	• Cost • Jobs
Campus	• Parking • Access to facilities • Traffic in and around campus • Uncomfortable temperature in classes

the taxonomic LSSM by incorporating additional data and insights about the student experience on campus. More formally, a concept model can be thought of as a set of categories (concepts) that have been inductively generated from the field data and then assembled into a larger meaningful whole through a set of relationships between them that have been identified interpretively. The concept model thus presents an insightful interpretation of a social situation; in the case of EMSS the social situation is student success on a particular campus.

FIGURE 2.8

An LSSM as a concept model for undergraduate students at a large public university in the Southwest. This simple concept model incorporates the taxonomy of barriers derived from a completed matrix along with the barriers belonging to each category of barriers.

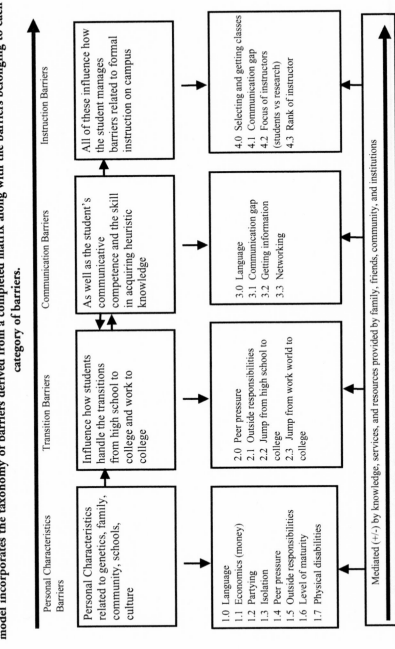

AUTOETHNOGRAPHIC ENCOUNTER: THE MIXING AND MATCHING OF THEORIES AND METHODS

Having decided during the 1980s to switch my research focus from dropouts to student success, I found myself in the unenviable position of lacking a theory and set of methods with which to undertake the proposed research. Resolving these problems launched me on a decades-long quest to find reasonable solutions. The answers came by degrees, with many twists and turns along the way. Fortunately, some of my doctoral students became interested in the issues, and in working with these students I was able to fashion new ideas and methods.

Convergent prior experiences also helped me to struggle with the issues. When I arrived at Arizona State University a few years before I began this research, most of my colleagues and their doctoral students in the Department of Higher and Adult Education were using quantitative methods to conduct research on student departure and other topics. Multiple regression analysis was widely used. Then students such as Stage (1986) began to use more sophisticated path analysis, and eventually, mirroring the field, students such as Pavel (1991) began to use structural equation modeling. These are powerful analytic methods indeed. But they were seldom accompanied by insightful theory. So in spite of powerful methods, little progress was made in the study of student departure.

At this time interest in qualitative research methods started to gain momentum. There was interest in the department in using such methods, so I was assigned the task of teaching the required introductory course in qualitative methods to doctoral students. In preparing to teach the course, I intensified my reading in qualitative research methods. As a result, I became familiar with the work of Miles and Huberman (1984), Spradley (1979), and many other researchers in various disciplines, including Glaser and Strauss (1967), Blumer (1969), and others. But I was particularly impressed by the analytic approaches suggested by Miles and Huberman. In a nutshell, they proposed a style of qualitative analysis in which the results would be displayed in either graphical or tabular form. This contrasted with the more literary types of qualitative analyses that had been done in the past. The literary-type analyses tended to create texts in which quotes from the data were liberally sprinkled. However, the reader always had to contend with the possibility that the author had not included all the relevant quotes, especially those that did not support the author's main arguments.

I was attracted to the methods of Miles and Huberman (1984) in part because I had already used a similar approach while doing my doctoral dissertation, which used qualitative methods long before they were popular in the field. In my doctoral work (Padilla, 1975) I organized all quotes in tables so that in presenting my arguments I could point to the tables as supporting evidence. This approach has the advantage that the reader can examine all the evidence along with the arguments. This allows the reader to judge the reasonableness of the arguments or to provide alternative interpretations of the data, if the reader is inclined to do so.

A problem I saw with the data display approach used by Miles and Huberman (1984), and inherent in my own previous work as well, is that when the tabular categories are created after the data are collected, it is likely that some of the cells in the table will have missing data. This can easily occur because while collecting the field data the researcher does not yet know what the data display will look like, that is, what the relevant categories might be. It occurred to me that the tabular display of data might be strengthened if the categories of data somehow could be identified before data collection. This thought was strengthened by the work of Spradley (1979), who proposed what he called "dimensional analysis" in his cognitively oriented approach to anthropological studies. In his approach, Spradley first identified key concepts from the field based on interviews with informants. He called these key concepts "cover terms" whose complete meanings could be unpacked by further interviews with informants. This systematic "unfolding" of meanings creates a rich semantic space that can be used to construct the informants' understanding of their life world.

What I needed was the cover terms that I could expand semantically with the help of informants to get at the black box campus experience. Fortunately, I had recently completed a qualitative study of high school dropouts that pointed to what I later conceptualized as barriers to continued enrollment and progress in school. These ideas were reinforced by the work of doctoral students such as Attinasi (1986) and Lowe (1989), who were doing related research. The first cover term that I identified was "barriers." But how is it that successful students are able to overcome all the barriers that come their way until they finally graduate?

I have had a longterm interest in computers, in fact, since I was in junior high school. When the first (later to be called) personal computer was prominently featured in the December 1974 issue of *Popular Electronics*, I was hooked immediately. It was the Altair 8800 microcomputer kit that was sold by MITS electronics. I bought and handbuilt that computer only to find out that it couldn't do very much for me because of its primitive features. A couple years later I handbuilt the Heathkit H-8 microcomputer (Heathkit was later taken over by Zenith, a successful computer vendor before IBM swept the market), and this machine I could use to do fun and useful things.

Following this interest in computers, I had been doing some reading in artificial intelligence and expert systems. I found the work of Harmon and King (1985) quite interesting, especially their understanding of expertise. It was then that it occurred to me that the successful students were able to overcome the barriers to success because they had become experts at being students. It was the work of Harmon and King that allowed me to go further and understand what such expertise might mean. (I have already described the basic ideas I incorporated from Harmon and King's work.) The concepts related to expertise provided an additional cover term, namely "knowledge" (actually heuristic knowledge). In other words, students can overcome barriers because they possess the knowledge that is necessary to overcome the barriers. Upon reflection, it became clear to me that having knowledge is necessary but not sufficient to overcome barriers. Students need to take action based on that knowledge if they are to actually solve problems and overcome barriers. So the third cover term had to be "actions."

As the cover terms were assembled in tabular form, it became clear that a matrix would form as the cover terms, following Spradley (1979), were semantically unfolded. Eventually, this process led to the term "unfolding matrix" to designate the method of data collection that uses this approach. It has the advantage that all the cells in the matrix can be filled with data, because the matrix is available before data collection begins. Since each cover term is a concept, the matrix actually encourages the saturation of concepts, as postulated by Glaser and Strauss (1967) in their grounded theory approach to qualitative research. The unfolding matrix also is handy for dealing with the issue of bounding of the data collection, a problem amply described by Miles and Huberman (1984). Here the problem is simply that, unless specific boundaries are set, it will not be clear to the researcher which are the relevant data to collect. Data collection without sensible limits is highly inefficient and may lead to data collection that is irrelevant to theory development.

Since I was originally asked a very pragmatic research question—how to help the sponsor increase student success—and I was about to launch a research project to capture the barriers, knowledge base, and action repertoire of successful students on campus, it occurred to me that merely identifying the barriers likely would not satisfy the sponsor. The sponsor was bound to ask about ways to reduce or eliminate the barriers. As I thought about this issue, it occurred to me that, if the students are indeed the experts on student success, then I should ask the students to suggest the changes the institution could make to diminish or eliminate the barriers. But it also occurred to me that changes can have both intended and unintended consequences: Why not ask the students to indicate what problems might arise if the institution actually were to make the suggested changes? This led to the expanded unfolding matrix, with two more cover terms: "changes" and "problems."

Over the years, as I have used the unfolding matrix, I always have been impressed by the capacity of students to understand why reasonable changes may not be doable given the problems that could arise if the changes were made. For me, this detail suggests an explanation as to why people can be more or less unhappy with their situation and yet continue to participate in it. They can identify some possible changes to improve things, but they also know that those changes may bring about unpleasant or unworkable circumstances. So a key to social change may be that, in the eyes of stakeholders, a proposed change needs to be viable, meaning that the change is feasible (doable) and that on the whole it would make things better than before, taking into account possible consequences resulting from the change. Call this a sensible attitude.

References

Attinasi, Jr., L. C. (1986). *Getting in: Chicano students' perceptions of their college-going behavior with implications for their freshman-year persistence.* Unpublished doctoral dissertation, Arizona State University.

Blumer, H. (1969). *Symbolic interactionism: Perspective and method.* Englewood Cliffs, NJ: Prentice Hall.

Glaser, B., & Strauss, A. (1967). *The discovery of grounded theory: Strategies for qualitative research.* Chicago: Aldine.

Harmon, P., & King, D. (1985). *Expert systems: Artificial intelligence in business.* New York: Wiley.

Lowe, M. (1989). *Chicano students' perceptions of their community college experience, with implications for persistence: A naturalistic inquiry.* Unpublished doctoral dissertation, Arizona State University.

Miles, M., & Huberman, A. M. (1984). *Qualitative data analysis: A sourcebook of new methods.* Beverly Hills, CA: Sage.

Padilla, R. V. (1975). *Chicano studies at the University of California, Berkeley: "En busca del campus y la comunidad."* Unpublished doctoral dissertation, University of California at Berkeley.

Padilla, R. V. (1994). The unfolding matrix: A technique for qualitative data acquisition and analysis. In R. G. Burgess (Ed.), *Studies in qualitative methodology* (Vol. 4, pp. 273–285). Greenwich, CT: JAI Press.

Pavel, D. M. (1991). *Assessing the fit of Tinto's model of institutional departure with American Indian and Alaskan Native national longitudinal data.* Unpublished doctoral dissertation, Arizona State University.

Spradley, J. (1979). *The ethnographic interview.* New York: Harcourt Brace Jovanovich College Publishers.

Stage, F. (1986). *University persistence: Motivational orientation within the Tinto model (attrition, achievement, student development, typologies).* Unpublished doctoral dissertation, Arizona State University.

3

STUDENT SUCCESS IN ELEMENTARY SCHOOL

Mary Miller

The purpose of this study was to look at a high-performing, high-poverty, high-minority (Hispanic) elementary school and at a school with the same demographics that was not performing at a high level, in order to study student success in both environments and to develop and compare a model of student success at each of these schools. In each school stakeholders (students, parents, teachers, and administrators) were asked to share their knowledge of what has contributed to student success in their school. The study resulted in the development of two contrasting models of student success.

The Expertise Model of Student Success (see chapter 2) was used to develop models for the two schools. Similar procedures were used to locate the site, select participant samples, and collect, date, and analyze them at each school. Based on data available from the Texas Education Agency, elementary schools with high poverty and high Hispanic student populations were identified. Schools were classified as "high Hispanic" when the population of this group exceeded the state average (42.7%) and "high poverty" when the percentage of low-socioeconomic students exceeded the state average (51.9%). The schools were classified as "high performing" or "not high performing" based on test performance data from the previous three school years. Because performing at the acceptable level is not considered low performance by the Texas accountability system, the schools in the second group were not identified as low performing. Instead they were designated "not high performing."

Sites

Two elementary schools were selected for this study. While both of the schools had high Hispanic and high poverty enrollments and were located in the same large urban area, one of the schools had consistently performed at high levels, while the other school had never exceeded the acceptable level on state-mandated tests. In this study, the high-performing school is referred to as Dale Evans Elementary and the not-high-performing school is called Woodview Elementary (both are pseudonyms). There were 100 participants in the study, including 47 students, 33 teachers, and 20 parents, all of whom completed their respective unfolding matrices. Each school's principal also was interviewed. Eighty percent of the participants were Hispanic, 8 percent were African American, and 12 percent were White, with the majority of the non-Hispanic representation coming from the teacher groups. Sixty-nine percent of the participants were females, with the female overrepresentation most salient in the parent group.

Data Collection and Analysis

For each campus, student, teacher, and parent groups completed unfolding matrices. The taxonomic LSSMs included both contingent and noncontingent analyses for the knowledge and action exemplars. The contingent analyses resulted in taxonomies for knowledge and action that were dependent on the prior barriers taxonomies. The noncontingent analyses resulted in taxonomies for knowledge and action exemplars that were analyzed cumulatively across each matrix. Only the results of noncontingent analyses are reported here. The unfolding matrices used in this study were expanded to include *changes* and *problems* cover terms.

At both campuses, unfolding matrices were completed with student, teacher, and parent groups. At both schools, all student participants were fifth graders, representing the highest grade level served at the elementary campuses. At Dale Evans, the three student focus groups had 11, 9, and 7 students, respectively, for a total of 27 students including 16 girls and 11 boys. Twenty-five of the students were Hispanic, one was African American, and one was Anglo. The teachers' group at this school consisted of 15 teachers. Three were fifth-grade teachers, 4 taught fourth grade, and 4 taught third grade; 1 taught students in the special education program, and 3 were support teachers. Seven were males and 8 were females. Nine of the teachers were

Hispanic and 6 were Anglo; this was representative of the staff as a whole. Nine parents participated at this campus. All 9 were Hispanic females.

Similar groups completed the matrices at Woodview. Two of the three Woodview student groups included 7 participants, and one had 6, for a total of 20 students. There were 13 females and 7 males. Eighteen were Hispanic and two were African American. Eighteen teachers participated at Woodview. These teachers represented all grade levels from pre-kindergarten to fifth grade except fourth grade, and also included support teachers. There were 14 females and 4 males. The teacher group included 11 Hispanics, 5 Anglos, and 2 African Americans. The parent group consisted of 11 participants and included parents and grandparents who were serving in the parental role. There were 9 females and 2 males; 8 Hispanics and 3 African Americans.

Overall, 47 students, 33 teachers, and 20 parents participated in the completion of the matrices at both schools combined, with the majority (80%) of the participants being Hispanic, well representing the population being studied.

Taxonomic LSSMs for Dale Evans Elementary

Barrier Taxonomies

Students at Dale Evans Elementary identified more than 30 specific barriers (see Figure 3.1) in response to the initial question, "What barriers does a successful student have to overcome to be successful, to get promoted?" Many of the identified barriers were personal problems that the students faced, including problems with peers, student behavior, and self-confidence. Students also identified barriers that relate to the outside world, including societal problems, such as drugs, race, and economics, as well as interests the students had that kept them from focusing on school, such as video games, sports, and television. Students identified some problems at home and some with their teachers, but overwhelmingly the barriers identified had to do with the students themselves.

Teachers at Dale Evans Elementary identified the barriers that they felt successful students at their school had faced and overcome (see Figure 3.2). While the student responses were very introspective, the teacher responses reflected deficit thinking, with the main focus on problems within the home

FIGURE 3.1
Dale Evans Elementary (High-Performing School): Barriers to Success Identified by Fifth-Grade Students

Societal Problems

- •Racial discrimination
- •Poverty
- •Drugs

Problems at Home

- •May be fighting with family or friends
- •Someone hurt or dies
- •Problems at home including alcoholism and abuse
- •May have to take care of brothers and sisters and have no time to study

Peer Problems

- •Too much peer pressure
- •Kids picking on kids
- •May be fighting with family or friends
- •People discouraging you
- •People bringing you down/blaming
- •Problems with friends talking about you/backstabbing
- •Showing off or thinking they're better
- •Having boyfriend/girlfriend or friends
- •People forcing you to do what you don't want to do

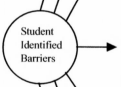

Student
Identified
Barriers

Teachers

- •Teachers sending students on errands
- •Having a bad teacher who doesn't teach right

Student Behavior

- •Staying up late/not enough sleep
- •Coming to school late or leaving early
- •Attitude
- •Immaturity
- •Their mouth
- •Distractions like eating candy in class or students passing gas on purpose
- •Not paying attention

Self-Confidence

- •Don't believe in self/no self-confidence
- •Worrying about how you'll do on test
- •Injuries or disabilities

Distractions

- •Video games/ TV
- •Because of sports or other things you do you may not be prepared
- •Worrying about sports
- •Worrying about how you look/fashion

FIGURE 3.2
Dale Evans Elementary (High-Performing School):
Barriers to Success Identified by Teachers

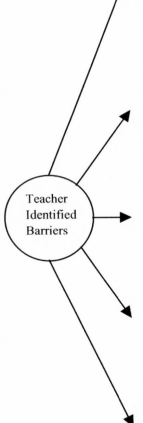

Home Structure

•Home life (divorce/going from home to home)
•Parents in survival mode
•Grandparents raising children
•Domestic infrastructure/home physical plant not conducive to homework
•Lack of structure in home

Home Support

•Lack of literacy in home
•Do not have materials at home for parents to teach concepts
•Parents do concepts differently
•Homework -- lack of help on it
•Parents sign off for work that students have not done

Academics

•Memory/Retention
•TAKS
•Language

Student/Teacher Relationships

•Student/teacher relationships
•Lack of respect for authority
•Students only work for rewards
•Bright students answer before less capable

Student Deficits (Lack of)

•Lack of confidence/self-esteem
•Lack of motivation
•Lack of interest
•Lack of experiences
•Lack of exposure
•Lack of sleep

Teacher Identified Barriers

and what the student was lacking. The home-related barriers that were identified were placed into two categories: those that dealt with the structure of the students' homes and those that related to the type and amount of support that was available in the home. In regard to structure, teachers viewed situations like divorce, lack of structure, grandparents raising the children, clashes between the home and school, and living in a physical plant that is not conducive to learning as barriers that successful students had to overcome.

In terms of support, the teachers identified many things that hindered parents in being able to truly help their children in the educational process. These included lack of materials for doing the work, lack of literacy in the home, parents doing concepts differently, and parents either not helping students with homework or signing off on work that had not actually been done. The teachers stated that successful students overcome lack of interest, experiences, sleep, exposure, confidence, and motivation. The teachers' own relationships with students also could be viewed as barriers: if students and teachers do not develop good relationships, if students do not have respect for authority, if teachers are not able to keep the brightest of students from impeding the learning of others, and if students are not intrinsically motivated and instead work only for tangible rewards. Only a few of the many barriers identified by teachers directly related to academics. These included (1) students' ability to remember and retain content, (2) overcoming the state test, and (3) language barriers (for students with limited English proficiency).

The third group that was asked about barriers to student success was the parent group (see Figure 3.3). Just as the teacher and student groups saw things differently, the parent group had yet a third perspective. Interestingly, their perspective focused more heavily on the barriers that the children confronted at school, including schoolwork, the teachers, and testing. Parents believed that schoolwork becomes a barrier when it is too hard, when the students do not understand it, or when they do not find it interesting or rewarding. The parents also identified problems when teachers were changed during the school year. They believed that such changes became a barrier that the students had to overcome. Parents also believed that a barrier is created when a personality conflict develops between the student and the teacher. Regarding academics, parents stated that students were pressured to pass the TAKS, resulting in student anxiety.

Figure 3.3
Dale Evans Elementary (High-Performing School): Barriers to Success Identified by Parents

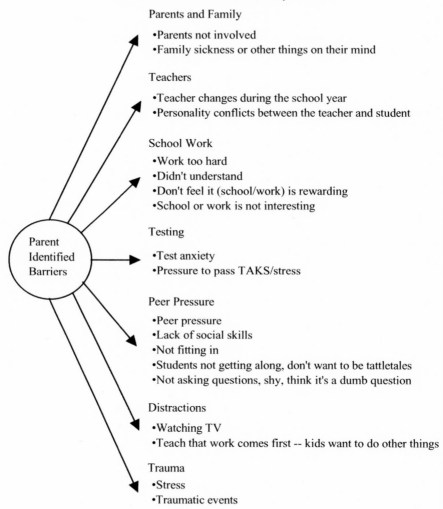

Parents and Family

- Parents not involved
- Family sickness or other things on their mind

Teachers

- Teacher changes during the school year
- Personality conflicts between the teacher and student

School Work

- Work too hard
- Didn't understand
- Don't feel it (school/work) is rewarding
- School or work is not interesting

Testing

- Test anxiety
- Pressure to pass TAKS/stress

Peer Pressure

- Peer pressure
- Lack of social skills
- Not fitting in
- Students not getting along, don't want to be tattletales
- Not asking questions, shy, think it's a dumb question

Distractions

- Watching TV
- Teach that work comes first -- kids want to do other things

Trauma

- Stress
- Traumatic events

Parent Identified Barriers

Like the students, the parents also saw peer pressure as a barrier for students. Unlike the teachers, who identified many problems at home, the parents stated only two: parents who were not involved and family sickness or other such problems that can interfere with the student focusing on schoolwork. The parents also recognized other things that interfere with students doing their best but that were not related to school or the home, such as watching television and serious trauma or stress in the lives of some students.

Although all three groups—students, teachers, and parents—were able to identify numerous barriers that must be overcome by successful students, the greatest number of barriers identified by the students were centered on the students' personal lives, relationships, and behavior, while barriers identified by the teachers related to home life and structure. The barriers identified by the parent group seemed more well rounded, encompassing some of the barriers of the other two groups but not focusing too heavily on any one type of barrier.

Knowledge Taxonomies

Based on a noncontingent analysis of the knowledge exemplars, a taxonomy of knowledge for the student data was developed as shown in Table 3.1. The taxonomy includes the categories of moral values, confidence, rules, consequences, truth management, attention management or focus, time management, and assistance or help.

For the teacher data, a taxonomy of knowledge was developed as shown in Table 3.2. The teachers believed successful students possess a wealth of knowledge that contributes to their success. Successful students possess academic knowledge, but they also have procedural knowledge in terms of organizing themselves, getting help, and using resources. According to the teachers, successful students also have personal knowledge of consequences and their impact in the future. While much of this procedural and personal knowledge may include things that the students learned in school, very little of it can be considered academic knowledge that students are expected to acquire in school.

The knowledge taxonomy for the parent data is shown in Table 3.3. Parents identified some knowledge that can be acquired at school. However, students also gain knowledge through life experiences. The categories of knowledge that resulted from the parent data include the following:

- Organization—Students know where to get help and how to manage their time.
- Personal—They know about self-confidence and understand that things will be different in the future because of their actions today.

TABLE 3.1
A Noncontingent Analysis of Knowledge Exemplars
Identified by Dale Evans Students

Knowledge Categories	Knowledge Exemplars
Moral Values	• Not supposed to be doing it • Shouldn't judge by looks • Know it's not nice • Trust, responsibility, privilege • Show respect • Everyone is equal • Color doesn't matter • Follow their heart
Confidence	• Have confidence • Believe in themselves • Do their best • Whatever happen, happens • "Gonna" get over it, figure it out • You may be different
Rules	• Not to talk when your teacher is talking • Be quiet during testing • Not to talk back • Don't hang with the wrong people • Don't do drugs • It's (drugs) against the law • Know that blackmail is against the law
Truth Management	• Know it's not true • Know to tell the truth • If it's not true it doesn't matter • Not important • Don't have to do it • People who treat you badly are not friends • They're making fun of someone else because they're not that good • Are bringing others down with them
Attention Management/Focus	• Do not think about it • Don't listen • Don't pay attention • Not to pay attention, ignore • Ignore, not let it get to you • Think about other things • Concentrate • Work hard • Have willpower • Know how to study • Relax / calm down / breathe • Control anger • Act normal

TABLE 3.1 (Continued)

Knowledge Categories	Knowledge Exemplars
Time Management	• Put a movie in to keep the children busy or give them naps, form play dates, or form a group • Do homework first • Don't procrastinate • Go to sleep early on test days • Follow a bedtime • Do the errand fast • Can say they don't want to do errand so they can stay in class • Only do the errand if you can handle it
Assistance/Help	• Tell the teacher • Can tell • Know to report the teacher so the teacher can be watched • Can talk about it • Talk it out • Counselor can talk about it • Can talk to parents • You can get help • Get comfort and help from parents • You can call Child Protective Services • Foster care, rehab, and support groups are available • There will be programs to help

- Help—Students know that help is available and that they should seek such help.
- Future—Students also have an eye on the future.

Action Taxonomies

The student, teacher, and parent groups were asked to identify the actions that successful students take by answering the question, "What does a successful student actually do to overcome each barrier?" The actions identified by students take many forms (see Table 3.4). Students confront some barriers on their own or by soliciting help from others. For other barriers, successful students see that ignoring the problem is the best way to address it. Still other actions include attention to scheduling and organizing oneself to deal with barriers as well as taking control of the situation.

Teachers identified student actions as finding and using resources to overcome barriers (see Table 3.5). Scheduling, using strategies, and having the right attitude also are important actions. As previously noted, teachers characterized student knowledge as knowledge about consequences, time

TABLE 3.2
A Noncontingent Analysis of Knowledge Exemplars
Identified by Dale Evans Teachers

Knowledge Categories	Knowledge Exemplars
Academics	• Have understanding of vocabulary, sentences, and nuances • How to manipulate both languages • Have a greater command of language • Life experiences • Know how to associate school content to more interesting things • Have interest in reading and writing • General inquisitiveness • See TAKS just like every test • Take TAKS as seriously as other tests • Know that both ways to do concepts can be good
Resource Management	• Take resources home • Take books home • Reader program • Public libraries • Internet • Newspapers • Take advantage of after-school challenge • Use a teddy bear, a buddy, or mirror to read to • Use the Internet at school
Help	• Teachers know there are brighter and slower students, who they are, and how to help each of them • Kids know that the teachers will support them • Parents help
Organizational Skills	• Organizational skills • Self-discipline • Behave differently in different settings • Know they have to do it • Get it done • Know they have to move on • Have to do more • Study habits • To write everything down • Use a homework calendar • Know they need sleep
Consequences	• Long-term consequences • Know consequences and that there are consequences • It will just make it harder if they are not respectful • Intrinsic rewards for being successful • Know to take a chance • Knowing it's all right to be wrong • Know they have another chance • Not the end of the world • Older children want to succeed to help the family • Doing right things for own needs
Future Orientation	• Know to take a chance • Knowing it's all right to be wrong • Know they have another chance • Not the end of the world • Older children want to succeed to help the family • Doing right things for own needs

TABLE 3.3
A Noncontingent Analysis of Knowledge Exemplars
Identified by Dale Evans Parents

Knowledge Categories	Knowledge Exemplars
Available Help	• Can ask for help from counselor, administrator, or another teacher to solve problem • They're not afraid to ask for help • That they can ask • Can raise hand • Additional tutoring • Parents understand work and can help • Knows there are other people to help • Support from home • Teachers are involved or other people • Teachers must make it interesting • Motivation from teacher
Attitude/Self-Confidence	• Get them involved, be a team player • Need to be more of a leader than a follower • Self-confidence • Happy with themselves • Go in with a positive attitude • Everybody is the same • Know that anxiety is normal • Know better coping skills • Possess more intrinsic knowledge • Know to do their best rather than expect A's • Competition • Challenging • Motivation
Time Management	• Prioritizing • Put work first • There is time for TV if work is done • Stay focused
Future Orientation	• Change happens, learn to embrace it, it can be good, not necessarily a negative • Rewards • Rewards come later • Things will pay off • Work may eventually pay off

management and organization, how to access help and the resources available, academic knowledge, and awareness of the future. Correspondingly, according to the teachers, student actions include organizing themselves, finding help and resources, being motivated to approach things with a positive attitude, and using strategies for academic success.

TABLE 3.4
A Noncontingent Analysis of Action Exemplars
Identified by Students at
Dale Evans Elementary

Action Categories	Action Exemplars
Get Help	• Tell teacher if kids pick on them • Tell the teacher that the other kids won't let you hear • Tell teachers if people are forcing you to do what you don't want to • Tell parent to report bad teachers • Confront person in charge of the teacher if the teacher is not teaching right • Tell teacher or counselor if there is alcohol or abuse at home • Talk to counselor about fights with family or friends • Ask for advice • Talk to someone who understands to get comfort if someone is hurt or dies • Need people to encourage and give them confidence • Find another babysitter—mom • Ask friends to help take care of brothers and sisters • Call Child Protective Services; report you are in an abusive situation • Call cops for help • Get help from available programs • Get support for injury or disability
Avoidance	• Ignore kids who pick on you or people who backstab • Ignore people who show off—they just want attention • Ignore people who try to force you to do what you don't want to do • Ignore their own disability • Ignore discouraging people • Try to get over it if someone gets hurt or dies • Break up if your boyfriend or girlfriend is getting in your way • Tell boyfriends or girlfriends you'll see them when you have time • Just say no to drugs • Walk away from backstabbers • Stay away from people who discriminate • Don't let a disability get in their way • Tell your mind to think about something other than the distractions • Don't worry about how you look • "Zip the lip" • Move away from friends in class to keep out of trouble • Try not to call (friends) • Learn not to fall to peer pressure • Have willpower and the mental ability to withstand peer pressure • Think about the consequences

TABLE 3.4 (Continued)

Action Categories	Action Exemplars
Take Control	• Control your attitude • Control how much time you spend on video games and TV • Talk to self or write in journal • Take deep breaths/ study/ think that they can ace tests • Have self-confidence • Try not to be self-conscious • Get knowledge about drugs and you won't do it • Get knowledge to help you mature • Watch the news • Grow up • Choose sports or something healthier • Do their best despite an injury or a disability • Kill those who discriminate with kindness • Apologize
Time Management	• Organize • Organization—set priorities—do one sport each day • Tivo favorite show and watch it in the morning • Don't stay up late • Try to go to sleep early • Study during week, do activities on the weekend • Time limits • Make up work
Confront	• Have a comeback like, "I know you are, but what am I?" • Confront person about fighting problem • Tell people who are forcing you to do something you don't want to leave you alone • Find out if they're really friends • Tell friends they don't like being backstabbed • Talk to friends who are backstabbing • Tell the teacher that they don't want to go on errands

According to the parents, successful students have knowledge in four major areas: confidence, time management/organization, knowing how and where to get help, and awareness of the future. They use their confidence to assert themselves in getting help as they continue to remain organized and focused on what they need to accomplish, as is shown by their actions (see Table 3.6).

All three groups agreed that successful students get help and resources to aid them in overcoming barriers. All three groups also agreed that successful students take the appropriate actions to organize and manage their time.

Changes to Lessen the Barriers

The students had many ideas about changes that the school could make to lessen the barriers. Although not many ideas were new, there were strong

TABLE 3.5
A Noncontingent Analysis of Action Exemplars
Identified by Teachers at
Dale Evans Elementary

Action Categories	Action Exemplars
Organize	• Make sure they have what they need in both homes where they stay • Find a space to work • Set up schedule on their own • Use free class time • Set goals
Use Strategies	• Use strategies until they become habit • Read and translate into first language to get better understanding • Use clues • Do over and over • Do it like the teacher taught • Read more • Go wash face to keep awake • Give detailed explanation • Bring up differences in (home and school) strategies in class • Try to assimilate and accommodate both home and school culture
Find Help/Resources	• Get breakfast and lunch at school • Meet basic needs at school • Gets needs from staff at school • Mentor • Willing to stay for help • Go on field trips to expand experiences • Talk to people, family, counselor • Find help • Will discuss at home • Get help from parents • Buy into rewards • Find things they're interested in • Seek out
Can Do Attitude/ Motivation	• Put nose to grindstone and work harder not to be a problem • Suck it up • No excuses • See big picture • See the test as motivating • Don't want to blow high standards • Take relationships personally • They don't expect something • Get satisfaction from earning an A

TABLE 3.6
A Noncontingent Analysis of Action Exemplars
Identified by Parents at
Dale Evans Elementary

Action Categories	Action Exemplars
Organize/Routine	• Have a routine that parents should enforce every day • Early bed/breakfast, rested • Prepare • Get things done correctly the first time so that you have more time in the end
Get Help	• Tell parents, counselors, or someone else • Speak to parents as a friend • Involve parents • Ask for help • Take advantage of tutoring and Saturday school—even for kids who don't need it • If they don't understand, they ask, even if it seems dumb
Assert Themselves	• Have a good heart-to-heart talk on the way to school • Communication is an important tool • They don't ignore it, instead they bring problems out into the open • Inform parents • Hook up with students with good social skills • Don't act shy • Have open mind • Give chance • Have self-confidence • Assume parent role
Focus	• Put problems aside and focus on work • Keep minds off problems at home • Don't let not fitting in bother them, instead it may motivate them more • Ignore peer pressure • Use imagination—see school work in another more interesting way • Do it because they have to

indications of areas where current practices needed to be modified or expanded. The most obvious area was discipline. Although it was clear that the school had a discipline plan in place, the students indicated that this plan should be strictly enforced. Suggested changes in this area included detention, enforcement of rules and consequences, putting students with strict teachers, giving more work, and having strict punishment. Students even suggested sending misbehaving students to first grade for the day or sending them to an alternative school or boot camp. At the same time that students wanted to throw the book at misbehaving students, they also suggested changes that were far more compassionate. The students suggested that the school should hire encouraging teachers (who could help the students by telling them to have confidence and that the work is easy), give students treats for good attendance, provide a sanctuary where students would feel safe, reach out to students, be more understanding, provide additional guidance, and add speakers and various supplementary programs. The students also suggested that changes in communication with parents would be beneficial.

Unlike the student group, the teachers did not recommend many changes in the way that student behavior was being handled. But (like the students) they recommended an increase in working with parents. The teachers recommended getting additional information to parents in the form of duplicate copies (when students split their time between two parents) and offering parenting classes, grandparent support groups, and GED classes. They also thought that parents could help their children more effectively if they had more events like Math Night, invited parents to observe how the teachers teach concepts so the parents could emulate them at home, and sent home sheets that told the parents how to do the homework.

Changes that teachers suggested should take place in the classroom included immersing children in a language-rich environment, having structure and routine in each classroom, and using appropriate vocabulary to get students accustomed to test-related words. Teachers thought that their own interactions with students could change by calling on students who were not answering and by greeting students in the hall and outside of the classroom to help establish rapport. Teachers also sincerely wanted to help the students and felt that they could do so by teaching some students how to create their own space. They also felt that provision should be made to see that all students get breakfast, even if a student comes in after breakfast has been served. The teacher group vacillated when it came to recognizing students. They believed that there should be more recognition, but they also believed that a policy of no tangible rewards might be best so that students could start to rely on the intrinsic value of learning.

The parent group had many ideas for changing the instructional practices to best meet the needs of the students. To support these changes, they thought that staff development should be provided for the teachers and that teachers who attend should be motivated and rewarded. These workshops would help them make their classes more interesting. Changes included making teachers more responsive to students, especially students facing difficulties. This may include allowing these students more time to complete an assignment, incorporating group work for students who are having difficulty understanding, or modifying the work. Parents believed that the teachers could change by better recognizing their students' needs and then accommodating them.

To increase parent participation, the parents suggested that meetings like PTA and social worker sessions could be scheduled at times when they could reach more parents, possibly at varying times throughout the year in order to reach both those who can attend during the day and those who can attend only in the evening. Consistent communication was seen as an important element of parental involvement. The parents wanted their children to have positive learning experiences and generally to feel good about being at school. They believed that this could be accomplished through the guidance program, through maintaining consistent discipline, and by adding some programs to help the students with their relationships.

Finally, the parents understood that sometimes there has to be change, but when change directly impacts students they thought a smooth transition is important. This included communicating with parents and students and allowing ample time for the transition to take place. The parents' suggestions leaned heavily toward providing programs and services to meet students' needs and increasing communication and parent participation in the education process.

One consistent theme across the three groups' proposed changes was the need to keep parents informed and involved in a number of ways. Although the school was already performing at a high level, each group saw that changes could be made to their school to make it even better.

Obstacles to Making Changes

After suggesting changes, each group was asked, "What problems might result if the changes were actually made?" Some of the problems they identified had to do with money, time, communication, and manpower, while others dealt with the usual resistance to change that may be encountered. Overall, the changes that students suggested would create minimal problems when implemented; these included changes that had to do with working with the students on a personal basis (to provide them with more guidance, support, and encouragement), talking to parents, helping students better manage their time, and sponsoring more speakers.

The teachers felt that many of their changes could be implemented without any problems, including creating language-rich environments, sending duplicate notes home, having outreach programs, introducing vocabulary to prepare students for tests, inviting parents to come to class to see how the teacher teaches a new skill, having grandparent support groups, teaching kids how to create their own space, greeting kids to build rapport, calling on all students who do not answer, and having more student recognition. Time and money were the biggest obstacles to other suggested changes.

The parents suggested that money, quick decisions, time, and communication were big problems for effecting change in the school. Some changes that could be implemented without much difficulty included student encouragement, an anti-bullying program, peer mediation, and more consistent communication that would help make parents more aware of how to help their children.

Taxonomic LSSMs for Woodview Elementary

Barrier Taxonomies

Students, teachers, and parents at Woodview Elementary participated in dialogical groups to complete the matrices that formed the basis for the taxonomic analyses at this school. The student group, like their comparable group at Dale Evans, was able to identify numerous barriers (see Figure 3.4). These included lack of effort, peer pressure, and a variety of distractions that students had to overcome. The majority of the barriers identified by the students dealt with the students themselves, including behavior, peer pressure, and effort. Only one of the major categories, academic challenges, was specific to the school. The last category, distractions, included personal distractions as well as issues relating to their homes.

The barriers elicited from the teacher group placed greater emphasis on home problems and outside factors, with a lesser focus on barriers related personally to the student (see Figure 3.5). The teachers identified only one category that related to the classroom, while all others related to things outside the school. According to the teachers, successful students have to overcome deficits present in the home as well as barriers related to the family

FIGURE 3.4
**Woodview Elementary (Non-High-Performing School):
Barriers to Success Identified by Students**

Academic Challenges

•Homework
•Testing -- difficult and hard
•Just don't get it (don't understand work)
•Don't get the work (can't decipher)
•Grades
•Don't have the help of others or parents
•Teachers' treatment (may not be fair)

Effort

•Your attitude
•Laziness
•Lack of enthusiasm
•Not paying attention
•Not listening
•Underestimation of self
•Lack of effort
•Not studying

Peer Pressure

•Peer pressure
•People make fun of smart kids
•Mean kids/kids who don't follow directions
•Bad friends
•People calling names
•Being like older brother (bad influence)

Behavior

•Behavior
•Playing around
•Cheating
•Talking
•Getting sent to the VP
•Cussing (gets them in trouble)
•Getting into fights
•Trouble
•Not being respectful
•Talking when someone else is

Distractions

•(Not doing) drugs, alcohol, cigarettes
•Asthma/illness
•Distractions
•Stuff at home (parents)
•Chores

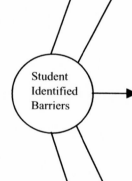

Student
Identified
Barriers

FIGURE 3.5
**Woodview Elementary (Non-High-Performing School):
Barriers to Success Identified by Teachers**

Economics

  •Money -- not enough or priorities
  •Economics
  •Moving
  •Role of mother has changed -- must now work

Home Deficits

  •Lack of parent involvement
  •Lack of family education
  •Lack of family valuing education
  •Lack of literacy in the home and is it valued?
  •Lack of real conversation
  •Stuck in rut/lack of education in home/not pushing for more

Family Structure

  •Children left alone
  •Broken families
  •Multigenerational families/family structure/community
  (Grandparents spoiling)
  •Overcrowded homes with multiple families living there
  •Parents not spending enough quality time with their children
  •Parents are too young
  •Fighting parents/spousal violence and abuse
  •Impact after family breakup
  •Unstable home/kids taking care of other kids

Teacher
Identified
Barriers

Classroom Problems

  •Teachers' low expectations of students
  •School behavior plan is needed
  •Student/teacher ratio
  •Too many levels in the classroom -- range from GT to
  special ed -- classes are at maximum enrollment (maxed
  out)
  •Too many disruptions

Exposure

  •Society -- exposure to TV and the times, sex, gangs, alcohol,
  drugs
  •Seeing sexual situations
  •Seeing drug use
  •Mature fast/early sexual attraction

Self Defeating Beliefs

  •Lack of self esteem
  •Overcoming stereotype that Hispanics will not succeed -- self-
  fulfilling prophecy
  •Acceptance of self-defeating things (pregnancies)

structure. Other problems cited included economic issues and exposure to negative elements. On a personal level, students were faced with overcoming their own self-defeating beliefs.

The parents saw multiple barriers in the school, an interesting contrast to the teachers' view of multiple barriers in the home (see Figure 3.6). Parents reported three categories of school problems: teacher actions, problems when two schools are combined, and academics. The parent group also identified peer pressure, as had been previously identified by the student group. They also mentioned problems that may exist between the home and school. Finally, parents identified health concerns as a barrier that successful students had to overcome.

Although all three Woodview groups—students, teachers, and parents— identified many different types of barriers, the student group seemed to focus more on their personal problems, the teacher group focused on problems that originated in the home, and the parent group noticed more problems within the school. In general, academic problems seemed far less pronounced than many nonacademic issues. Thus, knowledge for addressing these barriers does not necessarily need to be book knowledge but may be more heuristic.

Knowledge Taxonomies

A noncontingent analysis of the knowledge exemplars resulted in a taxonomy of knowledge for the student data (see Table 3.7). The resulting categories included knowledge of rules, perseverance, effort, consequences, time management, attention management or focus, and help. Among these categories, the students at this school seemed to have the most knowledge of consequences.

The taxonomy of knowledge based on a noncontingent analysis of the teacher data resulted in eight categories: aspirations or motivations, resources, the value of education, individual strength or independence, coping mechanisms, values and judgment, focus, and avoidance (see Table 3.8).

The noncontingent analysis of the vast amount of student knowledge identified by the parent group resulted in seven categories (see Table 3.9). These categories strongly related to knowledge that helps to guide students' actions toward success, including self-confidence, appropriate responses, healthy habits, study habits, self-control, avoidance, and help.

FIGURE 3.6
Woodview Elementary (Non-High-Performing School):
Barriers to Success Identified by Parents

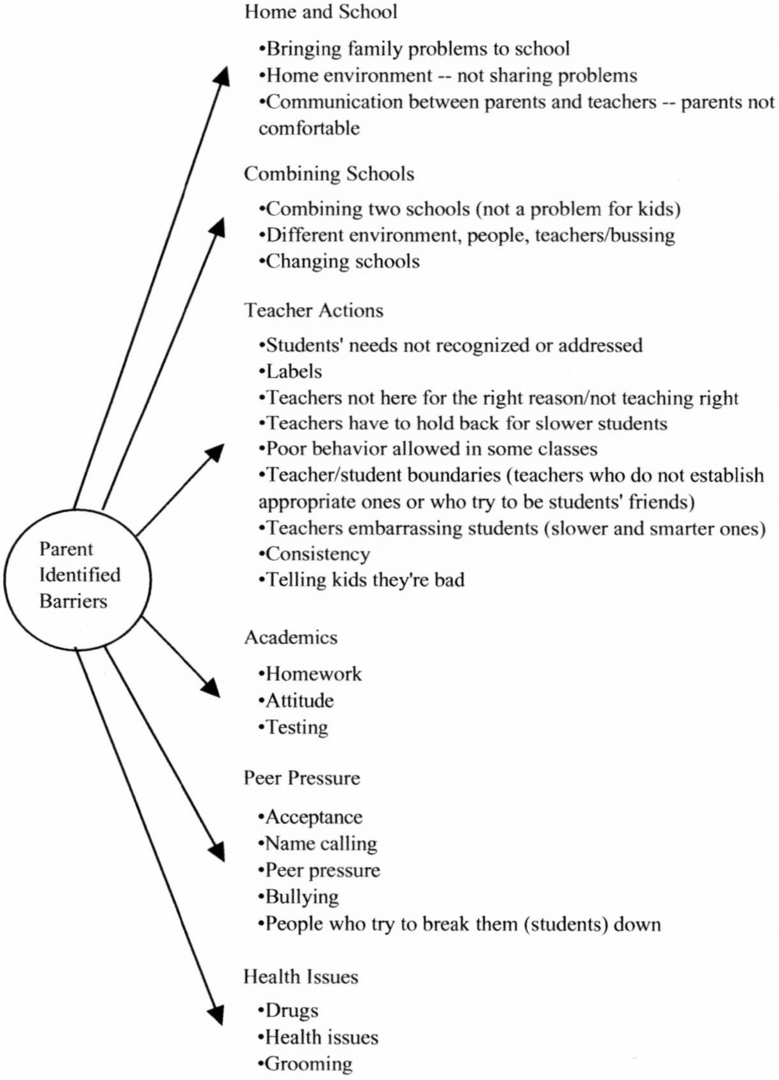

Home and School

  •Bringing family problems to school
  •Home environment -- not sharing problems
  •Communication between parents and teachers -- parents not
  comfortable

Combining Schools

  •Combining two schools (not a problem for kids)
  •Different environment, people, teachers/bussing
  •Changing schools

Teacher Actions

  •Students' needs not recognized or addressed
  •Labels
  •Teachers not here for the right reason/not teaching right
  •Teachers have to hold back for slower students
  •Poor behavior allowed in some classes
  •Teacher/student boundaries (teachers who do not establish
  appropriate ones or who try to be students' friends)
  •Teachers embarrassing students (slower and smarter ones)
  •Consistency
  •Telling kids they're bad

Academics

  •Homework
  •Attitude
  •Testing

Peer Pressure

  •Acceptance
  •Name calling
  •Peer pressure
  •Bullying
  •People who try to break them (students) down

Health Issues

  •Drugs
  •Health issues
  •Grooming

Parent
Identified
Barriers

TABLE 3.7
A Noncontingent Analysis of Knowledge Exemplars
Identified by Woodview students

Knowledge Categories	*Knowledge Exemplars*
Rules	• Know to pay attention to what teachers say • Not to cuss • Stay out of places where they know they'll get in trouble • Playing around is not being respectful
Perseverance	• Perseverance • Don't let anything hold you down • If you don't believe in yourself you won't pass and you won't have friends • Other students may make smart kids do their homework, but they should be firm and not do it • You know that you don't like teachers who are not fair
Effort	• Try their best or they won't get it • Try hard • Try their best/study • In order to succeed you have to put in effort • Challenge • Keep grades up
Consequences	• Drugs affect people's minds • Drugs slow down what you are doing • You could die from drugs • Drugs may force you to do things that are not right • Drugs get you into trouble • Won't get lesson or understand and not listening if you are talking • If you talk when someone else is, you won't know what you're doing or what the teacher is saying • Won't know how or what to do • Playing around will get you in trouble • If you fight you will go to principal • Behavior leads to too much in trouble • Too much time in office • Spend time in vice principal's office, won't get work done • If your attitude gets out of hand it will get you in trouble • Playing around is going to get you in trouble • You won't know answers • If you follow a bad influence you will be in trouble • Teacher or principal will catch you cheating • You're hurting yourself • Not using your own knowledge • Peer pressure makes life harder • Big brother has problem if he tries to get you in trouble
Time Management	• Do homework every day/turn in when due • Do both today's chores and tomorrow's • Study when you have extra time • Try not to miss school

(continued)

TABLE 3.7 (Continued)

Knowledge Categories	Knowledge Exemplars
Management/Focus	• Ignore people who make fun of smart kids, they're probably jealous • Ignore problems • Distractions can help focus on what you're doing/keep mind on what you are doing • Focus even though you're not feeling well • Pay attention • Believe that problems at home will pass • Play around outside instead of in class
Help	• Ask teacher • Try to help solve problems • Get tutored • Know to take medicine to keep you well

Action Taxonomies

Students were able to identify numerous effective actions for overcoming barriers (see Table 3.10). Overwhelmingly, the students attempted to avoid many of the problems that they encountered on a regular basis, whether at home, in school, or in their personal lives. When they could not avoid barriers, students sought help from others. They also exhibited many positive actions indicating that they displayed good behavior and had a strong work ethic, good study habits, healthy habits, and a positive attitude.

The noncontingent analysis of action exemplars identified by the Woodview teachers demonstrated many positive and proactive actions, including thinking and acting positively, looking for opportunities, making good decisions, getting help from others, finding resources, exercising self-discipline, taking initiative, and having a strong work ethic (see Table 3.11). In addition to these actions students also appear often to not take action or to avoid situations, resulting in a category of avoidance behaviors.

Parent-identified actions showed that successful students find ways to succeed despite how the teacher acts or the type of pressure and problems that they encounter. When the noncontingent analysis was completed for the parent data, six categories resulted: avoidance, getting help from others, study habits, healthy habits, self-confidence, and positive thoughts and actions (see Table 3.12).

When the action categories identified by students, teachers, and parents were compared, some convergences among the three groups were found; however, there are still many actions that were identified by only one of the

TABLE 3.8
A Noncontingent Analysis of Knowledge Exemplars
Identified by Woodview Teachers

Knowledge Categories	Knowledge Exemplars
Aspirations/ Motivation	• They want more • There is something better out there • They don't want to do the same thing their family has • Know they don't want to leave their children alone like parents did • Look outside the box • Things will get better • Their parents want more for students • Want to change (overcome negative stereotypes) • Motivation/drive • Motivation • Self-motivation • Have personal goals • Many express that they want to be teachers • Language and conversation—don't want to be like their parents • Prove society wrong about self-defeating things
Resources	• Outside influences—church • Exposed to good examples • Join groups • Get praise • Help is out there • Wider environment • Know good role models that are not family members • To attach themselves to others—some call teachers their parents • See teacher more than parents • Young parents can't help so they look for other resources • Will ask teacher for necessary supplies • Background knowledge • After-school program is available
Value of Education	• Their parents respect teachers and appreciate the opportunity • Someone impressed students with the value of education • Know importance of education • Education is the only stability/constant • Be more determined to learn • Teach younger kids • Stay in school

(continued)

TABLE 3.8 (Continued)

Knowledge Categories	Knowledge Exemplars
Individual Strength/ Independence	• Feel good about self • Know what they're good at • Have good problem-solving skills • Use computer • Love reading—may be an escape and may motivate in other areas • Read on their own • Independence • Self-discipline • Got to do it your own way • Maturity • Self-motivated • Self-motivation and discipline • Find their own place
Coping Mechanisms	• They have a coping mechanism • Knows how to cope • Patience • Feel safe at school • Will adapt • Switch dependency to someone else other than family • Get values from grandparents instead of parents
Values/Judgment	• Know who's bad • To look away, shut their eyes to the things they're not supposed to see • To learn from mistakes of others • Know what to do • OK to go against society • Moral values
Focus	• To focus on work • Know where the focus should be • Know what's important • Tune out disruptions • Go to room and study or read
Avoidance	• To stay away from trouble • Weed out the bad • Don't play with bad kids

groups. It was clear that all three groups felt that successful students use avoidance as an effective strategy for addressing many of the barriers. All three groups also saw that successful students ask for help. All agreed that successful students think and act positively. There was agreement between the student and parent groups on two additional action categories, study habits and healthy habits. Between the student group and teacher group there was agreement on work ethic. *Good behavior, look for opportunity, make*

TABLE 3.9
A Noncontingent Analysis of Knowledge Exemplars
Identified by Woodview Parents

Knowledge Categories	Knowledge Exemplars
Self-Confidence	• Students believe in self • Self-confidence • Have self-confidence when dealing with peer pressure • Have self-confidence to be accepted • Knows he'll make new friends • Knows he'll make it / He can do it • Knows he doesn't have to fit in • "I don't fit in" • Knows that some people are labeled • It's not true if someone says they are bad
Appropriate Responses	• Knows how to respond to name calling • Make right decisions • Be a positive leader • Be friends with less fortunate • Knows to be polite to other kids • Communicate with other parents with different boundaries • Can take over for teacher
Healthy Habits	• Exercise • Do what others kids do to stay healthy • Not give up on health • To take care of himself • Grooming is important • Have to take responsibility for own grooming • It's important to learn and teach and for parents to know about drugs
Study Habits	• Needs to study, go to library • Listen, understand, and ask questions • Knows how to use a homework diary • Do their best • Study • Go to bed early • Eat • Prepare • Understand homework to pass test
Self-Control	• Self-control • How far to go with poor behavior • Know how to judge boundaries • How to get by when students are not behaving in class • It's up to him whether or not to let someone bring him down • How to push buttons

(continued)

TABLE 3.9 (Continued)

Knowledge Categories	Knowledge Exemplars
Avoidance	• Overlook name calling • Not to bring family problems to school • Stay away/ignore • Knows it's a teacher problem not a student concern • Knows the changes in the schools are temporary
Help	• Get help from parents • Knows to get counseling, put worries at different level • Go to counselor • Everybody needs someone

good decisions, find resources, self-discipline, take initiative, and *self-confidence* were identified by only one of the groups.

Changes to Lessen the Barriers

After reflecting on the barriers that had been identified, each group was asked to suggest changes the school could make to help lessen or eliminate the barriers. Most of the student-suggested changes fell into one of five major categories: time management, additional services, monitoring, discipline, and positive reinforcement, with parent contact and homework being additional categories. In the area of time management, students felt that some changes could be made to ensure that the teachers cover the entire curriculum prior to tests being given. They felt that this could be accomplished by giving the teachers more time to teach, either by decreasing nonteaching duties or by lengthening the school day. They also felt that the school should look at its homework policies and see if there could be a balance so that there would not be too much homework for one class or on one particular night. They felt that students also would do better if they could stay longer after school to get more help.

Most of the services students requested were already in place; however, the students felt that there was a need to justify more of these services, particularly more help for students learning to deal with their temper. The students felt that changes should be made in the discipline practices in the school. They believed that students who misbehave should receive harsher consequences, which included "getting rid of the bad kids," separating those who break the rules, knowing when to remove a student from class, suspending students, sending them to alternative programs, and having zero tolerance. The students also advocated for an increase in monitoring, suggesting

TABLE 3.10
A Noncontingent Analysis of Action Exemplars
Identified by Students at Woodview Elementary

Action Categories	Action Exemplars
Avoidance	• Walks away from drugs • Gives drugs the cold shoulder • Just say no • Get rid of bad friends • Tell bad friends that you don't want them • Stay out of places where trouble might be • Avoid people who will get you into trouble • Stay away from people playing around and ignore those who do • Walk away from fights • Try not to cause a fight • Tell principal about fights • Ignore name calling • Walk away from name calling • Don't cuss • Ignore distractions • Stay away from pressure • Don't talk to kids who are pressuring them • Walk away from peer pressure • Ignore bad influences • Stay away from areas where bad influences are • Tell others to be quiet or talk to you later • Ignore those who are talking • Don't care about mean kids • Avoid mean kids • Ignore mean kids
Good Behavior	• Don't talk when teacher is talking • Listen carefully to instructions and follow them the first time • Do what you're told • Behave • Pay attention • Be quiet • Make up or skip cuss word • Do what you're supposed to do • Stay in place instead of moving around and playing • Better restraint • Control • Try to behave better • Act like the kids the teacher is treating better • Better themselves, not be in a bad situation • Tell other students that misbehavior will hurt grade

(continued)

TABLE 3.10 (Continued)

Action Categories	Action Exemplars
Asking for Help	• Ask how to do the work • Ask teacher for help and directions • Ask another student for help • Ask for help at school if no one can help at home • Ask teacher if parents can't help • Ask teacher for help if you were not listening • Ask teacher or others when you don't get the work • Ask for extra help • Ask to be moved away from mean kids • Talk to counselor—try to get it out of your mind • Talk to teachers or counselors • Tell teacher about distractions • Tell teacher on mean kids • Tattle tell when they're in danger • Stay after school
Work Ethic	• Don't be lazy • Do your best • Try your hardest • Do chores immediately • Work hard on chores • Know what I know (and don't need to cheat) • Do my best • Use knowledge in mind • Change it (enthusiasm) • Don't be lazy • Do best • Do work
Study Habits	• Try to do as much homework as possible • Study and use the computer • Do their homework • Study • Know they have to study so they do • Read over chapter • Take notes • Follow instructions • Read carefully • Work out problems • Use good strategies and methods • Use computer to make work easier and faster • Study, pay more attention • Try over if they don't get the work • Read again

TABLE 3.10 (Continued)

Action Categories	Action Exemplars
Healthy Habits	• Outside play and exercise • Get body moving • Get energy • Sleep early • Use a pressure ball to relieve feelings
Positive Thinking	• Be optimistic • Remember good things and compliments • Don't give up even if you don't have help at home • Ignore problems at home and try to do something fun • Ignore illness (don't let it get the best of you) • Believe in yourself • Have dignity • Change attitude • Try to be different (attitude-wise) • Take chances • Be assertive • Talk to bad influences about what they are doing • Don't be simple-minded

that this could be accomplished by putting cameras in the classrooms, having more people monitoring, having parent volunteers walking the hallways, and checking for weapons.

Students also felt that some of the barriers could be addressed by taking a more positive approach, such as more recess, doing activities that would "give kids energy," having a party for students who exhibit good effort, and encouraging students to try their best. They also suggested an increase in parent conferences.

Like the student group, the teachers saw the need to improve campus discipline. The teachers stated that a consistent behavior plan was needed that would result in action being taken when students are sent to the office. They felt that the addition of an in-school–suspension teacher would be a worthy investment. At the same time, the teachers' intent was not merely to punish the students; they also wanted to provide them with helpful services. They believed that more counseling was needed as well as other services, such as tutoring and afterschool programs.

The teachers felt that the school could build on the existing parental involvement program by offering more training, including GED classes. They thought that, if the school could make these classes more convenient in terms of time and also provide food and childcare, they would have more

TABLE 3.11
A Noncontingent Analysis of Action Exemplars
Identified by Teachers at Woodview Elementary

Action Categories	Action Exemplars
Think and Act Positively	• Positive attitude • Make the best of their family situation • Look for uniqueness • Hang around more positive role models • Aspire to be positive
Look for Opportunities	• Hang around educated people • Migrate to intellectual children and adults • Hang around more positive role models • Look for opportunities • Determined to learn and to help their parents • Go for it (education) and grab it immediately • Find better pursuits like sports and hobbies • Try to find areas where they can be successful
Make Good Decisions	• Make good decisions • Do the right thing • Avoid situations • May choose not to have kids • Are more selective about the TV they watch • Be responsible • Schedule time more effectively
Self-Discipline	• Use self-discipline when facing problems in class • Use self-discipline to get out of family rut • Set own goals • Make do with what they have • Well-behaved
Get Help from Others	• Seek out other role models • Seek out friends to talk to • Find other adults to be proud of them • Ask office to intervene • Talk to grandparents or teachers • Inform parents • Do things with their parents • Stay with teacher • Get attached to someone safe
Find Resources	• Find other resources • Look for resources • Make own money • Take books home

TABLE 3.11 (Continued)

Action Categories	Action Exemplars
Take Initiative	• Take initiative and become peer tutor • Take initiative • Ask for extra work • Ask for extra help • Become leaders • Become the adult • Do projects • Work on ongoing project • Develop survival skills
Work Ethic	• Drive • Work harder • Work harder at something they're good at
Avoidance	• Ignore • Move on • Occupy mind with other things • Block it out • May become loners

participants. The teachers showed interest in being more involved in parent training so that they could teach parents about how better to help their children in classes.

The teachers believed that the school should be doing something to address mobility by trying to convince families to stay and finish out the year whenever possible. They also were in favor of having a consistent school district curriculum since many of their students moved within their district. They also felt that if they put families in touch with community services it might keep them from having to move so often.

The teachers felt that changes were needed in the structuring of classrooms. Teachers thought that they could do their job more effectively if they could lower the student-to-teacher ratio. They knew that this would require the hiring of more teachers but believed that, if this could be done, they might be able to (1) avoid split classes (in which one teacher has a class containing two grade levels), (2) have more homogeneous groupings and thus better address all student instructional needs, and (3) departmentalize by content area. They wanted to be able to hire a teacher for the "gifted and talented" students. The teachers believed that all of these changes would help them to address the multiple needs in their classrooms and to better serve their students.

TABLE 3.12
A Noncontingent Analysis of Action Exemplars
Identified by Parents at Woodview Elementary

Action Categories	Action Exemplars
Avoidance	• Ignore name calling • Walk away from name calling • Turn other cheek to peer pressure—right and wrong • Don't talk about home problems in school • Turn away from drugs • Hide/cope on their own
Get Help from Others	• Get help from parents if the teacher is not teaching right • Ask for help in the right way if needs are not being met • Ask questions • Talk to counselors, friends if they have problems at home • Approach teacher or principal for help with bullying • Report to parents or teacher teachers who are embarrassing students • Talk to volunteer parents or counselor about home problems • Tell adult that teacher has no boundaries • Have parent approach administration about teacher/student boundaries • Get their parents to go to the teacher about student's level, grades, attitude • Talk to principal about class behavior • Ask to be moved within room or to another room • Make friends • Communicate and make friends
Study Habits	• Prepare • Study for test • Practice • Go to bed early before test • Do own homework • Do it (homework) • Teach at child's level
Healthy Habits	• Have a positive attitude • Exercise • Take action on own to groom self • Look at friends for grooming ideas • Eat • Go to bed early before test
Self-Confidence	• Stand up for self • Prove yourself • Don't accept label • Know who you are
Positive Thoughts and Actions	• Follow rules • Be more like the teacher and establish boundaries • Be polite • Keep trying • Try to improve • Have a positive attitude

Changes proposed by the parents echoed some of the changes previously mentioned by students and teachers and added a few new ideas. Like the previous groups, parents suggested changes in discipline. They too wanted stricter rules and for the teachers to be more vigilant in curtailing incidents of peer pressure and bullying. They called for additional programs, including counseling, tutoring, and incorporating health and wellness activities into the school day. The parents advocated training, particularly for teachers but also for administrators who should be monitoring the teachers. They also suggested increased monitoring of discipline by teachers and increased monitoring of teachers by administrators, including cameras in the classrooms.

The parents thought the teachers could change some of their strategies in order to better meet student needs, including small-group instruction, testing students when they enter, and using more time to teach and less to test. Parents suggested that teachers adjust the type and amount of homework given to enable them to help children at home on their homework. The parents encouraged more listening, especially to children who are having problems at home and those who are being bullied at school. Parents felt that there should be an increase in the number of motivational activities that help children feel good and make them less susceptible to negative labeling.

Perhaps the greatest change the parents called for was an increase in parent and teacher collaboration and the development of relationships between these two groups. They wanted additional activities in which they could participate but they also wanted more communication between themselves and their children's teachers. As stated succinctly by this group, "Teachers and parents need to bond." This bonding may occur through open house activities, parent volunteers in the school, or sending notes home. Regardless of the format, the parents felt that this was a big change that needed to happen in the school.

Each of the three groups was able to identify changes that could take place to make Woodview a better school with fewer barriers and more successful students. Three commonalities emerged across groups: Increased discipline, better interactions between parents and teachers, and increased services for students.

Obstacles to Making Changes

Woodview students, teachers, and parents had several ideas for making their school a better place to learn. But the groups at Woodview also were able to see what problems the suggested changes might cause if actually implemented. One of the main problems identified was that some changes may cost too much money to implement. They also thought that their get-tough policy may negatively affect morale. Some of the changes also could create new problems, including parent opposition to the change. Teachers recognized that they had limited time and much to do, which could impede the realization of many of the suggested changes. Budget, time, and planning were identified as primary issues along with getting people to buy into the changes.

Attitudes also were a concern, as was communication from teacher and parent groups. Parents felt that some of the changes could be met by resistance from the teachers, while recognizing that much of what they were proposing would cost time, money, and manpower. Transportation, money, and staff may not be available for many of the initiatives, but a bigger problem may be acceptance of desired changes. Overall, the major obstacle to change came down to available resources (money, time, and people) and attitude.

LSSM Concept Models

Three primary resources were used to synthesize the concept models for the two elementary schools: the various taxonomies already described, interviews with the school principals, and Padilla's (personal communication, February 1, 2005) conceptualization of the "golden triangle of education" (GTE). Interviews with the principals provided a means for triangulating the taxonomic data. They also provided an opportunity to reflect on the data so that a broader interpretation of the situation could emerge.

According to Padilla (personal communication, February 1, 2005), schooling can be thought of as a framework for creating a "golden triangle of education." Each side of the triangle represents one of the primary stakeholders, namely, students, teachers, and parents. The GTE is intended to accomplish two main goals: to school the students and at the same time to rear them. While the teacher's main role in the GTE is to school the student while the parents' main role is to rear their child, on some occasions the teacher needs to act like a parent and rear the child. Likewise, on some occasions the parents need to act like a teacher and school the child. The GTE is effective if everyone carries out his or her role effectively. If the teacher or parents fail in their schooling and child-rearing roles, the child's schooling and rearing are likely to suffer.

Although the principal is not a primary stakeholder in the GTE, the principal exerts great influence over what occurs within it. More generally, it can be said that all stakeholders in education outside of the primary stakeholders in the GTE are attempting to influence what happens inside of the GTE. The GTE is used as a central feature of the LSSM concept models presented in this section.

Concept Model for Dale Evans Elementary

Principal's perspective.

When interviewed, the Dale Evans principal stated, "it's going to be an alignment of these two groups [parents and teachers] that's going to have the greatest impact on student success." He pointed out that, although a school can be very successful and can be working "extremely hard" and "parents can be working hard with their kids," "whenever these two [parents and teachers] align is when you are going to have the ultimate growth." The principal believed that the goal of any successful school is getting the parents and teachers all working on the same side and realizing that they are on the same side. After this has occurred, he said, "Conquering these problems over here [the barriers identified by all of the groups] is a whole lot easier."

When asked to identify barriers to student success in his school, the principal responded, "outside interferences, society, the way a lot of them have to live, home life, and some testing pressure that creates the stifling of good solid instruction." When asked more about what he meant about home life, he clarified that it was directly related to the economic status and not attitudes or perceptions of the parents of the families: "It's just their unfortunate circumstances that they're having to survive in." These comments reinforced many of the comments made by the teacher group.

When asked about the behavior and discipline in the school, the principal explained that in many cases they tried to get the kids to discipline themselves. With regard to teacher discipline he stated, "They're really good at motivating the kids . . . they [the students] know that the teachers and myself care about them and we have expectations for their behavior and that their goal is to help themselves become successful."

When looking at the barriers that the students identified, the principal felt that a lot of those things were things the school was teaching. He said,

"I'll tell you one thing about successful schools. You can't assume that core values that a human being should have are being taught at home." He also felt that people in school have to get excited because "too many people at home don't have time to get excited." He stated that this should not be taken for granted.

After looking at the knowledge exemplars that students, teachers, and parents identified, the principal agreed that, although all categories of knowledge listed were important, the root is the child's moral values. He talked about how "they" wanted to keep church and school separate and admitted that, "I don't know if I cross that line sometimes or not." He did believe that "It takes a village to raise a child," and that principals need to be allowed to stay at a school for a long time so that they can establish such villages. Building a relationship with parents is also part of being at a school over time. He spoke of how "sometimes it's just letting the parents know that you're not on a pedestal" and how in his own experience parents initially had that impression. He said that perceptions are something that have to be dealt with, and he felt that this school was beyond initial perceptions to where a working relationship had been formed.

The principal thought that the knowledge needed to be successful at Dale Evans was accurately depicted. This included the moral values that he believed were critical for student success. While it had been suggested by one group that the school get rid of rewards, the principal spoke a lot about intrinsic motivation, naming one particular teacher who excelled at pulling out the rewards from within the students; the students did well because they wanted to please themselves, not the principal or the teacher, and to create their own success. Also in regard to the students' knowledge, the principal said, "The academics are all taught by the teachers; you're not born with them. Morals and all that, that's what's missing sometimes. They have to have a core stem of knowledge. Most of the teachers work on this all of the time."

In regard to actions taken by successful students, the principal pointed out that "The kids seemed to have a big understanding of what it's going to take to be successful." He talked about how the values built a good foundation, saying, "If you have a good foundation, everything is going to go from there. As parents, if we build a strong foundation, even though it cracks from time to time, it's going to hold strong." He pointed out that every "kid" is going to have to go out and experience things for him- or herself, and thus will encounter barriers. "It's the kid who doesn't have the foundation that doesn't recover."

Concept model.

Examination of all the barriers identified by Dale Evans students, teachers, and parents, along with the principal's input, resulted in three major types of barriers faced by students in this school: interactions, deficits, and distractions. In terms of interactions, students must contend with peer pressure, behaviors around their friends and in school, and their relationships with teachers, family members, and friends. The deficits category includes students' own deficits, whether in terms of lack of skills, knowledge, or experiences, lack of self-confidence, things that are lacking in their homes, and real or perceived individual deficits. With regard to distractions, students were sometime distracted by their own behavior or that of others and by many societal, school, and family problems. The students' ability to filter through distractions, overcome deficits, and engage in positive interactions is a strong indicator of their potential for success.

Students must address interactions, deficits, and distractions coming at them from four sources: personal, home, school, and society. To address these types of barriers, successful students at Dale Evans used the vast knowledge that emanates from their being schooled and reared in the GTE. At this school, the golden triangle of education is grounded on moral values. The evidence derived from the dialogical groups shows that successful students at Dale Evans have strong moral knowledge, including knowledge of values, rules, consequences, and truth, that helps them navigate the barriers. This knowledge, when combined with their practical knowledge in time management as well as their use of both human and nonhuman resources, helps students to overcome barriers. Successful students act on their knowledge to assert themselves and take control of their situation. Their action is guided by strong moral values, some of which the students may have brought from home and some of which may have been learned in school.

The Dale Evans concept model for student success (see Figure 3.7) begins with the students entering the school to experience a geography of barriers consisting of interactions, deficits, and distractions (emanating from home, school, personal, and societal issues). As the students experience school, they engage the GTE. At Dale Evans the GTE was grounded on strong moral values and exhibited coherence among the students, teachers,

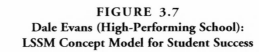

FIGURE 3.7
Dale Evans (High-Performing School):
LSSM Concept Model for Student Success

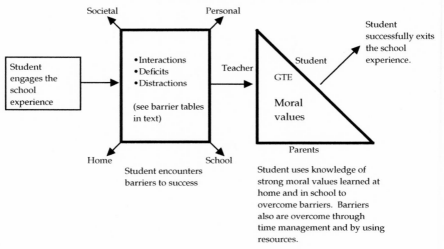

and parents, enhanced by the positive influence of the principal. The high degree of coherence resulted in an effective GTE that served as a solid foundation for the school. The students brought strong moral values to their schooling experience and combined them with time management skills and the use of resources to overcome barriers and successfully exit the school experience.

Concept Model for Woodview Elementary

Principal's perspective.

The Woodview principal thought that the data derived from the dialogical groups accurately portrayed the campus, pointing out that the students focus on themselves because "they're told that so much." She also stated, "The teachers will always blame the home, but how do we overcome that? Those are things that we cannot change; the only thing we can change is ourselves and our attitude towards the child and the family, and then from there we can work systematically to correct or assist; we can never change it, so what do we do about that instead of just complaining?" The principal also concurred with the perspective of the parents, stating, "And I can see where the parents, in their mind, put a lot of blame on the teacher and the administration because in their view we are not doing enough for their child."

Additional barriers that she felt the three groups may not have included prompted her to say, "The successful student I think has overcome many barriers; the reality of our situation is the home life here, and I am not just talking about here but in every district. The home may be a multigenerational home, may be a broken home; there may be problems there. I think a lot of times if the student has good role models in the school they can overcome; if we give them the assistance I think they can overcome just about any outside barrier."

The principal felt that the knowledge identified by the groups in her school represented her students and stated, "I think it's more than just consequences, but if the children know where to get help, I think that's one of the priorities for me because the rest will all fall under that." She then prioritized knowing how to get help as more important than the other exemplars identified by the group.

The focus on consequences among the students was proportionately much greater than the rest of the data. When asked what accounts for this, the principal explained, "Because teachers tell them they are going to have consequences. One of the things I have not been able to change here is . . . the teachers' attitude so when students break the rules we should focus on positive behavior. All students want to please, even the student we see in the office every day, and yet teachers still decide that negative consequences is the best, punishment is the best, where I see we'd get better results if we did positive reinforcement instead."

Regarding knowledge identified by teachers, the principal stated, "If I had to prioritize right now at this point, I'd probably say resources. I really, truly believe that if a person is truly interested in that student and showed that, they could turn that child around, any child. I've seen it happen." In response to the parents' thoughts on student knowledge, the principal added, "What I found here and something that parents can truly help are two things, study habits and self-control." After reviewing all of the knowledge exemplars, the principal commented that she was surprised that the parents had not mentioned the value of education, stating, "I would have imagined that parents along with teachers would have said that they value education. Maybe that says something about what the teachers were saying about what is going on in the home." The conversation then turned to blame. It appeared that the teachers blamed the home and the home blamed the school and the students blamed themselves. To this thought the principal responded, "Isn't that odd and of all people they shouldn't be blaming themselves; as a child they have very little control."

When asked to review the actions that successful student take, like avoiding trouble, having good behavior, study habits, asking for help, and thinking positively, the principal responded, "That's good, and that's from the kids. They know! I would say yes, exactly, I agree with them." When asked which of these she felt was the most important, she returned to study habits. The principal talked about how schools focus so much on good behavior and staying out of trouble instead of focusing on good study habits. She also explained how students don't always know how to ask for help. She talked about the importance of thinking positively and keeping up their health. She also pointed out that grades don't always represent the abilities of the students and may instead be more related to their behavior, saying, "You know what else I've found? Sometimes teachers give good grades to students who behave good, and if a student misbehaves and if he's a thorn in your side and everything, their grades do not [*sic*] reflect it and it's not necessarily so," meaning that the grades do not reflect the abilities but instead reflect the behavior. The principal pointed out that this is more common in the lower grades, where there is not as much grade accountability as in the upper grades due in part to the absence of a state-mandated standardized test at this level.

When reviewing the actions that the teachers identified, the principal seemed a bit perplexed, pointing out that everything was "behavior, behavior, behavior, and having good ethics." She stated that the kids were more on the mark, even though one might have expected that the teacher group would be more in tune with what was happening. The principal observed that this study showed that the teachers perceive behavior as the most important thing when it should have been academics. She said, "Obviously the teachers feel like they [students] need to behave good, then they are going to be academically successful. . . . I don't think that's necessarily true." She further pointed out that there was a higher degree of correlation between the student and parent groups than with the teachers: "Students and parents are very similar, and the teachers not, shows you what they're stressing. I think some of our teachers just miss the consistency part. Many teachers give mixed messages and they don't know."

When examining the changes that were suggested by all three groups, the principal stated that she needed to be "tougher!" She pointed out how the law does not always allow you to be as tough as some may wish. The principal stood by her assertion that, if students are taught where to get help and if they learn good study habits, they will be able to go far. She thought that discipline should be done in a more positive manner instead of punitively.

Concept model.

The barriers identified by Woodview students, teachers, and parents were taxonomized using the same categories as in the comparison school, namely, interactions, deficits, and distractions. Although the specific barriers may differ between the two schools, both schools face similar types of barriers. Consequently, the concept model for the non-high-performing school begins in the same manner as for the high-performing school (see Figure 3.8). While both models begin in a similar manner, one portion of the two models is quite different, namely the dynamics of the GTE.

For the high-performing school, an effective GTE exists. That is, there is a high degree of coherence of beliefs among the parents, teachers, and students. These beliefs are rooted in moral values. At Woodview the GTE is grounded in discipline. However, the Woodview GTE does not exhibit sufficient coherence, so it does not provide an effective foundation for schooling. This does not mean that a school grounded in discipline cannot be a successful school. It could be if the GTE were coherently applied. While all of the stakeholders at Woodview agreed that discipline is important at the school, inconsistency emerged regarding the form that discipline should take. Students consistently blamed themselves or their peers for lack of discipline, teachers blamed the families, families blamed the teachers, and the principal admitted that she had not been able to establish the type of discipline philosophy that she believes would work best in the school.

It appears that at Woodview the teachers set the tone for the climate that focuses on disciplinary success as a means to achieve academic success. Students enter the school bringing some discipline from home and acquire more in the school. In order to succeed in school, students use this discipline along with avoidance strategies, asking for help, and maintaining positive thoughts. Unfortunately, due to the incoherence of the GTE and the principal's admitted inability to change the dynamics of the GTE with regard to discipline, the number of students experiencing success was limited, and many students were falling through the cracks.

As Figure 3.8 demonstrates, the GTE for the non-high-performing school shows that Woodview's parents, students, and teachers, although seemingly focused on the same goal of achieving student success in their school, often work against each other or pull in different directions instead of working as one cohesive unit. This provides a weak foundation for the school to do its work. This does not mean that some students cannot move through this model and achieve success. Both schools have successful students. But because of the lack of a coherent GTE, the Woodview students have a less effective support system that results in fewer students who are successful—at least as demonstrated by scores on state-mandated tests.

Summary of Comparison

The research at these two schools revealed that schools with similar demographics can face similar barriers. It also showed that some students in each

FIGURE 3.8
Woodview (Non-High-Performing School):
LSSM Concept Model for Student Success

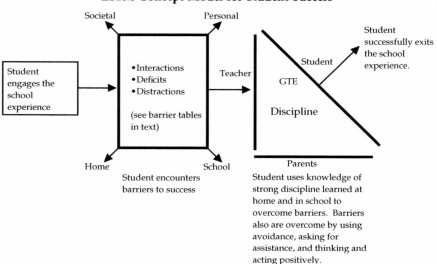

school can possess relevant heuristic knowledge and take effective actions to overcome barriers. How students deal with barriers in their respective schools greatly depends on the coherence of the GTE and in particular the beliefs on which the school is grounded. At Dale Evans, the goal was for students to possess a strong knowledge of right and wrong and to adhere to a high moral code. The teachers focused on making changes that would increase communication and interactions in order to help the students be successful. The parents sought additional programs and other ways to get their children's needs met. The students at Dale Evans, like those at Woodview, were highly focused on discipline but also saw the need for support and services to help them. At Woodview, it is evident that all three groups (students, teachers, and parents) were focused on discipline, but each from their own point of view. Teachers expressed dissatisfaction with the way student discipline was handled, and parents saw a lack of cohesion between parent and teacher groups when it came to working together for the students.

The lack of cohesion at Woodview was accompanied by some finger pointing that was not apparent at Dale Evans. A degree of separation between the parents and teachers at Woodview also was noted, as was the principal's inability to have a positive, unifying impact on the school's GTE. The principal could detect the deficit attitude of the teachers but was unable to change it. The teachers—instead of the principal, the community, or the students' needs—seemed to drive the model of the school. There also was a noticeable difference between the parent groups at the two schools, with the Dale Evans group appearing more knowledgeable and supportive of the curricular programs at the school, while the Woodview parents, although supportive of a quality education, appeared more concerned with discipline and self-esteem.

Implications

With the increase in standards and accountability movements throughout the country, it is more and more important that schools have large numbers of students performing at high levels. This is particularly the case in schools serving the growing Hispanic population and those serving low-socioeconomic populations. Both of these groups historically have underachieved. Current research and existing theories fail to adequately explain the differences in performance between Hispanics or students from impoverished backgrounds and the middle-class White population, nor do they provide specific directions for how to ameliorate this problem.

The findings of this study provide support for earlier compatibility studies. Garcia (2001) states that, the more compatible the organization is with the home, the more likely the school can enhance student learning. Such compatibility was evidenced at Dale Evans Elementary, where a high degree of cohesiveness was found between the home and the school—resulting in a high degree of student success. Effective-schools research has repeatedly signaled the importance of the parent and school relationship. This study once again reveals that cohesiveness between these two groups enhances success, and further illustrates that when there is a lack of cohesiveness, as was the case at Woodview, minimal student success is achieved, and students' needs may not be met. The findings of this study further support previous research showing that the achievement of students with similar backgrounds varies considerably based on school practices and that schools can have a significant impact on student achievement (Dufour, Dufour, Eaker, & Karhanek, 2004). Even though similar populations of students may encounter similar barriers, schools can make a significant difference in promoting student success.

Economic issues also are reflected in the barriers evident in the two schools studied. Although student success, or lack of it, often is thought of in terms of students failing to achieve on standardized tests or other academic indicators, this study showed that many of the barriers students must contend with are directly or indirectly related to their economic situation. Because economic condition plays a pivotal role in many of the barriers encountered by students in high-poverty, high-minority schools, educational practices can be greatly influenced by economic policies. Often schools are charged with solving problems related to student success that actually have little relation to educational issues. As the Hispanic and low-socioeconomic populations continue to grow, especially in states with high minority enrollments such as Texas, it is important to clarify the role that schools are expected to play in the context of a changing student population. Is the school's role to solve educational problems or to address societal issues? Can these two be separated, or must they remain closely bound, as they were in the two schools studied?

Policies need to take into account not only how money is distributed to schools but also how much flexibility schools will have in spending it. The roles and responsibilities of the schools must be taken into consideration. Funds allocated only for instructional programs will not provide schools the resources to adequately address the nonacademic needs of the students. Without addressing those needs, the students will not be able to achieve higher standards but will suffer the punitive consequences of the educational accountability system.

Like much research that has stressed the importance of leadership (Carter, 2001; Davis & Thomas, 1989; Lezotte, 1991), specifically in the principalship, this study illustrates the impact of the principal on school performance. Because the principal influences the GTE, districts must ensure that they hire and train highly qualified instructional leaders who are able to detect what is driving the GTE for their school. They must have the ability to influence the GTE by advocating instructional practices that facilitate success. Davis and Thomas (1989) and Lezotte (1991) both highlight the importance of the principal setting the tone and communicating the mission. This study illustrates differences between a high-performing school in which the principal was able to do this and a non-high-performing school in which the principal admitted that she was not able to positively influence the practices that drove the GTE for the school.

It is a given that just about all students will encounter some barriers on entering school. This study has shown that the knowledge that students use to deal with these barriers is most often heuristic knowledge. Consequently, closer examination of heuristic knowledge is merited, as it seems that through use of this knowledge students are most able to overcome barriers. Because of high-stakes testing, schools spend much time developing the skills and strategies needed for success on tests, which often neglects the heuristic knowledge and skills students need in order to get through school successfully. The heuristic knowledge that students require is school dependent, so support programs for student success must take that campus dependency into account.

Although poverty is the most consistently noted indicator of poor academic achievement, Evers, Izuni, and Riley (2001) and Stringfield and Land (2002) have pointed out that the relationship between informal knowledge and school performance is twice as strong as the relationship between family income and performance. While students from high-poverty backgrounds may come to school with limited experiences, it does not mean that schools cannot be constructed to give students the experiences that they need to be able to construct their own knowledge. To do this, schools must reexamine their curriculum to determine if it is designed to provide students, especially poor and minority students, with the rich experiences that they need. Too often high-stakes testing or something else drives the curriculum, which may result in a watered-down curriculum. The high-performing school in this study showed attempts to provide students with a rich experience, believing that the motivation elicited by such activities enhanced the student's desire to do well in academic areas.

AUTOETHNOGRAPHIC ENCOUNTER: APPLYING EMSS IN AN ELEMENTARY SCHOOL SETTING

Too much of the existing research focuses on school failure, so schools spend time focusing on eliminating failure instead of increasing success. Research, and often the accompanying dollars, tends to focus on the higher levels of education. This results in limited attention to the primary school years when the odds of being able to impact struggling students are the highest. At this level there has been less time to develop huge gaps in achievement between successful and struggling students, and greater parental support exists for students during these early years. Unfortunately, while schools should focus on achievement, most operate in a remediation mode, especially in schools with high minority and high poverty populations. The Hispanic population is growing in unprecedented proportions, and yet success of Hispanic students lags behind that of the White population. All of these concerns were critical in my decision to study this particular population at the elementary school level.

Seeing schools with virtually the same type of students, and yet one school was highly successful while the other was not, inspired many "why" questions about what was happening in these schools. If one school could have success with a certain population, why couldn't another school? What was happening in each of these schools to promote (or not promote) success? Upon hearing of the "black box approach," I wanted to know what was in the "black box" of certain schools, namely those that were successful versus those that were not. When introduced to Padilla's EMSS, I discovered a framework for answering this question.

Understanding that EMSS had not been used previously with elementary school students gave me the opportunity to apply an extant model to a group of students that had rarely been studied. This held great appeal for me. Because there was no previous use of EMSS with young students, the incorporation of other stakeholders in the process (teachers and parents) was a necessary precaution in case elementary students were less verbal than high school and college students. What resulted was rich student data that were augmented by teachers and parents, adding multiple, yet related, perspectives. True to the old adage "from the mouths of babes . . ." it proved to be a telling way to study student success in an elementary school. It revealed what was happening in some schools that enhances student success, and what could potentially happen in all schools to increase success for many more students.

References

Carter, S. C. (2001). *No excuses: 21 Lessons from High-performing, high-poverty schools.* Washington, DC: The Heritage Foundation.

Davis, G. A., & Thomas, M. A. (1989). *Effective schools and effective teachers.* Needham Heights, MA: Allyn & Bacon.

Dufour, R., Dufour, R., Eaker, R., & Karhanek, G. (2004). *Whatever it takes: How professional learning communities respond when kids don't learn.* Bloomington, IN: National Education Services.

Evers, W. M., Izumi, L. T., & Riley, P. A. (Eds.). (2001). *School reform: The critical issues.* Stanford, CA: Hoover Institution Press.

Garcia, E. E. (2001). *Hispanic education in the United States.* Lanham, MD: Rowman & Littlefield.

Lezotte, L. W. (1991). *Correlates of effective schools: The first and second generation.* Okemos, MI: Effective Schools Products Ltd.

Stringfield, S., & Land, D. (Eds.). (2002). *Educating at risk students.* Chicago: University of Chicago Press.

4

STUDENT SUCCESS IN A HIGH-MINORITY HIGH SCHOOL

Kimberly S. Barker

The purpose of this study was to examine high school student success. Following the EMSS framework discussed in chapter 2, the study identified the barriers perceived by high school students along with the knowledge and actions that students used to overcome those barriers. Additionally, the investigation explored the extent to which the perceptions of those who are in charge of ensuring student success (i.e., teachers, counselors, and administrators) were consistent with the barriers perceived and articulated by the students themselves. Specifically, the study addressed the following questions:

1. What do students perceive to be the barriers to successful completion of high school?
2. How do students overcome these perceived barriers? Specifically, what does a successful student know and do to overcome each barrier?
3. What do teachers, counselors, and administrators perceive to be the barriers to successful completion of high school? Specifically, what do these individuals believe are the knowledge base and action repertoire of successful students?
4. Are the perceptions of teachers, counselors, and administrators consistent with student perceptions of successful high school completion?

5. What are the implications of the match or mismatch between the perceptions of students and those of school personnel?

Understanding the answers to these questions has the potential to reveal pertinent information that can be used to enhance school success for all students.

Site

The site selected for this study was a high school located at the edge of a large city in south central Texas. Demographic data about the site came from the Texas Education Agency, specifically the online Campus Profile of the Academic Excellence Indicator System for 2002–2003 (Texas Education Agency, n.d.). The subject school serves grades 9 through 12.

The student population of this school (approximately 1,200) was high minority. The district reported 81.2 percent of its students as Hispanic, and a large portion of the students (66.7%) were economically disadvantaged. However, only 2.7 percent of the students were limited English proficient (LEP). While the completion rate of the school was close to the state average, school district personnel desired improvement in this area.

The participants included a sample of high school seniors, teachers, counselors, and administrators. Four groups of 6 students (a total of 24) were interviewed, in separate group interviews lasting approximately 45 minutes each, to complete an unfolding matrix. The students represented an ethnic and gender mix of twelfth graders selected from English classes. As with the student sample, four groups (of 4 to 5 teachers, for a total of 18) were interviewed, in separate group sessions lasting approximately 45 minutes each, to complete a second unfolding matrix. The teachers represented an ethnic and gender mix, as well as a wide range of subject-matter and experience levels.

In addition, three counselors and three administrators were interviewed individually. Participants were chosen based on the school principal's recommendation and on availability. Both men and women, Hispanic and White, were selected. Each was interviewed separately for approximately 45 minutes. The counselor and administrator interviews provided feedback on preliminary models of success developed from the data provided by the students and the teachers. The purpose of the counselor and administrator interviews was to provide triangulation of perspectives in order to improve the robustness of the findings.

Taxonomic LSSMs

As shown by the taxonomic LSSMs for the campus, the study points to substantial forces that can obstruct the path to high school graduation for many students. The complex range of barriers identified indicates that past history and cultural, social, and environmental factors work together to create diverse student educational needs. Student and teacher perceptions of barriers overlapped in some areas. However, there were some areas of disagreement. Additionally, there were both parallel and divergent views among students, teachers, counselors, and administrators concerning some issues. The following sections will reveal the student- and teacher-identified barriers to student success at this campus, followed by counselor and administrator perceptions concerning those barriers and their relationships to the student and teacher data.

Barrier Taxonomy for Student Data

The barriers from the student responses were collapsed into five categories as follows: (a) distracters, (b) lack of motivation, (c) negative peer pressure, (d) lack of resources, and (e) systemic failure (see Figure 4.1).

Distracters.

The distracter barriers include a diverse set of barriers that the students perceived as stumbling blocks on the path to successful completion of high school. The majority of the barriers in this group involve commitments and relationships with other people, which the students find difficult to manage and control. The barriers categorized as distracters reflect some of the external forces on the students that they may have difficulty controlling and managing. All of the student groups adamantly voiced that raising a child, problematic relationships at school and home, and job commitments work against the student's ability to concentrate at school. While the barrier of being overcommitted to extracurricular activities was voiced as a distracting obstacle, the participants generally viewed this hurdle as easier to overcome than the other barriers previously noted.

Lack of motivation.

All of the student groups noted that being motivated is a major factor leading to student success. The values and internal forces that shape a student's

FIGURE 4.1
Barrier Taxonomy for the Student Data

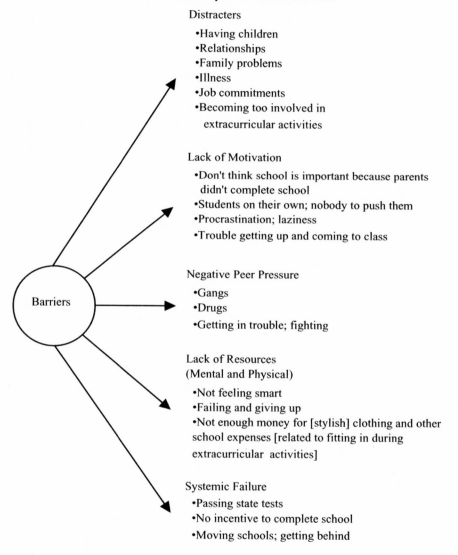

Distracters
- Having children
- Relationships
- Family problems
- Illness
- Job commitments
- Becoming too involved in extracurricular activities

Lack of Motivation
- Don't think school is important because parents didn't complete school
- Students on their own; nobody to push them
- Procrastination; laziness
- Trouble getting up and coming to class

Negative Peer Pressure
- Gangs
- Drugs
- Getting in trouble; fighting

Lack of Resources
(Mental and Physical)
- Not feeling smart
- Failing and giving up
- Not enough money for [stylish] clothing and other school expenses [related to fitting in during extracurricular activities]

Systemic Failure
- Passing state tests
- No incentive to complete school
- Moving schools; getting behind

Barriers

beliefs can determine whether or not a student graduates from high school. The foremost barrier in this category comes from students devaluing school and not thinking it is important for their future success. The participants mentioned that sometimes that belief comes from the home. In other words, the parents and other relatives do not believe that school is important. This is a critical problem, because "students on their own" and/or with "nobody to push them" face an uphill battle to graduate from high school. The students connected motivation to the value of school. Students who think school is important are motivated to attend school. Once at school, though, there are additional barriers, such as negative peer pressure.

Negative peer pressure.

The students clearly articulated the components of negative peer pressure. Involvement with gangs and/or use of illegal drugs is a barrier to successful school completion. The peer pressure to join gangs or use drugs is found by some students to be an enticement from which they cannot disassociate. According to the participants, not being able to avoid this barrier leads one down a disastrous road of crime, jail, and even death. Another type of peer pressure that the participants noted is "getting in trouble" and fighting. The students revealed that troublemakers tend to continue their bullying and threatening behavior even after being disciplined, creating a school climate of fear for some students. This barrier interferes with school success when students' worrying about safety preempts learning.

Lack of resources.

This group of barriers includes both mental and physical challenges to obtaining adequate resources needed for success. The participants stated that students' "not feeling smart" strongly impacts their ability to perform well in school. In other words, the student's own self-image plays an important role in success. Students who do not feel smart are likely to seek nonacademic avenues to improve self-esteem. Those students who make poor grades sometimes give up on school, feeling it is a futile effort. The participants mentioned that students who fall behind a grade level miss being in classes with their friends and lose interest in school. After failing, they give up and leave school rather than stay behind and try to complete high school with another graduating class. This barrier is identified as a lack of mental resources, because the students feel mentally inadequate to perform the tasks necessary to graduate.

The other type of resources that students may lack includes "not enough money for [stylish] clothing and other school expenses [related to extracurricular activities]." The participants noted that this is an important issue among those families trying to stretch low income as far as possible. Looking fashionable at school is so important to some teenagers that they would rather not go to school than be at school dressed in old or outdated clothes. Additionally, the participants mentioned that the costs of various school-sponsored extracurricular activities can sometimes dissuade students from joining. Students without monetary resources are sometimes left on the fringe of being able to become involved with school. This leads to the final category of barriers to school completion, that is, systemic failure, which includes obstacles to graduation that the school system places in the pathway of its own students.

Systemic failure.

School systems do not purposefully set out to erect barriers to school completion. However, all the student groups mentioned that passing state tests as a prerequisite to graduation is a task that is daunting and insurmountable for some students. The students did not disagree that minimum knowledge standards are necessary for the school system to control the quality of its graduates. The group participants indicated that the barrier exists because not all of the students receive the same degree of preparation for these tests. "By the end of the day," one student said, "the teachers are tired and just rush through the lesson. They don't remember that it is the first time we have heard it [the material]." Even though the school offers test-tutoring classes before or after school and individual teachers offer test tutoring, the students indicated that those sessions are difficult to attend due to scheduling conflicts that prevent going to school early or staying after school. For example, those students who ride the bus are not able to attend morning or after-school tutoring sessions. Also, the group participants explained that the students who have work commitments after school are not able to attend afterschool tutoring and are too tired to attend early-morning sessions.

Along with the testing barrier, another systemic barrier that the students perceived to be an obstacle to school completion encompasses the curriculum offered at the school. Several students mentioned their disappointment with the course selection offered at the school, stating that there is "no incentive to complete school" if courses that interest the students are not offered. A course specifically noted to be of high interest but not offered at the school is cosmetology. The participants maintained that more course offerings that are at a high interest level among the students would create an increased connectedness to school and give students more incentive to stay in school and complete their high school diplomas.

A final barrier to school success in the systemic category deals with inconsistencies in the presentation of course materials among schools and districts. The barrier of "moving [between] schools," which causes students to "get behind," is an obstacle that faces students who change schools. Since different schools lack alignment in course content, any student who must change schools is at a potential disadvantage concerning the new school's level of coursework. The participants stated that students who get behind as a result of changing schools find it almost overwhelming to try to catch up with the new class and frequently give up due to the enormous frustration. Even if teachers offer tutoring to these students, not all students can or will take advantage of the extra help needed to bring their skill levels up to the required level. Thus, students who move and change schools face the dilemma of an American school system that is not academically consistent among districts, regions, or states.

Knowledge and Action Taxonomies for the Student Data

The taxonomies for knowledge and action for the student data were created based on the taxonomy of barriers already described. For each category of barriers the corresponding knowledge and action exemplars for each barrier in that category were collected. The resulting taxonomies of knowledge and action are shown in Table 4.1. Technically, these taxonomies are based on a contingent analysis of the knowledge and action columns of the unfolding matrix. The knowledge and actions pertaining to each barrier category are described in the following sections.

Distracters—Knowledge and actions.

The students emphasized the importance of successful students being knowledgeable about the seriousness of their decisions. "Know the consequences [of poor decisions]" and "know right from wrong [concerning getting into trouble]" are two of the statements that students made about some of the distracter barriers. Having a vision also is important, as indicated by the students' comments, "know what you really want [for yourself]" and "it's important to finish high school." According to the participants, the successful students know that difficulties are not something that can be totally avoided, as evidenced by statements such as "don't let problems get to you," "being

TABLE 4.1
Knowledge and Action Taxonomies for the Student Data

Barrier Category: Distracters

Knowledge
- It's important to finish high school
- Know what you really want [for yourself]
- Know the consequences [of poor decisions]
- Know when you need help
- Know right from wrong [concerning getting in trouble]
- Understand that you will lose the trust of teachers and administrators [if you get in trouble]
- Being around trouble-makers is inevitable
- Don't let problems get to you
- It's difficult to make a work commitment and find time for studying and friends

Actions
- Be involved in organizations
- Stay at school more
- Finish high school
- Set goals
- Don't become too serious [with romantic relationships]
- Use birth control or abstinence
- Move in with relative if it [home life] gets really bad
- Act adult/mature
- If needed, get help from an administrator

Barrier Category: Lack of Motivation

Knowledge
- Know that it [success] is up to them [students]
- Know that they [students] should make something of themselves
- It [success] is an individual effort
- Be mentally strong
- Be self-disciplined
- Start early; you can relax later
- The more you wait, the less you want to do it [complete schoolwork]

Actions
- Think about goals
- Push yourself
- Prioritize
- Do what you need to do first
- Do not follow in parent's footsteps [if they did not complete school]
- Move in with [supportive] relative

(continued)

TABLE 4.1 (Continued)

Barrier Category: Negative Peer Pressure
Knowledge • Education comes first • Know that peer pressure is powerful • Know not to get involved in gangs • Know that gang involvement is not worth it • Learn from others who have gone through [mistakes of drug use] • Limit yourself to what you can handle
Actions • Don't join gangs • Stay away from gang members • Get involved in sports, ROTC, family, or charity work [to avoid pressure to join gangs] • Don't even start [illegal] drug use • Spend money on better things [than drugs] • Stay away from people who use drugs • Get help from teachers
Barrier Category: Lack of Resources (Mental and Physical)
Knowledge • Education is the most important • Have confidence [in yourself] • Have mental toughness • Know to study more • Keep going [don't give up] • Know that there is summer school [to catch up] • Know that [stylish] clothing and other expenses are only temporary [concerns]
Actions • Find something you're good at and get involved in it • Take summer school, if needed • Get extra help from tutoring—teachers or friends • Study extra • [Take] extra notes • Don't worry about [not having enough money for clothing and other expenses] • Get a part time job

TABLE 4.1 (Continued)

Barrier Category: Systemic Failure
Knowledge
• Finish school
• You can make more money with a diploma
• Know it's [state testing] important
• Take practice tests seriously
• Pay attention in class
• Make some good friends [good role models]
• Jump in as fast as you can [when trying to catch up on work]
Actions
• Look forward to the future
• Think about what can happen later on [after graduating]
• Study
• Take practice tests as often as possible
• Meet new people
• Talk to teachers separately
• [Attend] tutoring after school to catch up

around troublemakers is inevitable," and "know when you need help." Successful students also perceive the importance of preventing problems when possible: "it's difficult to make a work commitment and find time for studying," "understand that you will lose the trust of teachers and administrators [if you get in trouble]."

Along with this knowledge, the student participants revealed the actions that successful students take in order to overcome the distracter barriers. These actions include "act mature/adult" enough to "set goals" and have the mindset to "finish high school." According to the student participants, these actions lead the way to conscious decisions concerning relationships, such as "don't become too serious [with romantic relationships]," "use birth control or abstinence," and "move in with relative if it [home life] gets really bad." The participants noted that many successful students deal with distracters by "stay[ing] at school more" and by using school organization membership/ involvement as a means of escaping distractions. "Be involved in organizations" is emphasized as a way for successful students to surround themselves with other successful students and receive positive guidance from the adult organization supervisors. If problems persist, the students stated that the successful students will know to actively seek help from an adult in order to resolve the problem. "If needed, get help from an administrator" is one student's suggestion. The knowledge and actions revealed by the student participants provide insight into the methods that successful students use in order to overcome the distracter barriers.

Lack of motivation—Knowledge and actions.

To reach the goal of high school graduation, successful students must have a core of knowledge about motivation and an ability to act upon that knowledge. The student participants revealed that the successful students are those who possess key personality traits that allow them to "be mentally strong" and to "be self-disciplined." These students believe that they are in control of their future, as evidenced by the statements that successful students "know that it [success] is up to them" and "it [success] is an individual effort." Underlying this knowledge is the belief that "they [students] should make something of themselves" and that being successful in school is a pathway to that result. The group participants also mentioned that the ability to not procrastinate is essential for success, stating that successful students know that they should "start early," with the knowledge that they "can relax later." As far as completing schoolwork goes, the successful students know that "the more you wait, the less you want to do it." These bits of knowledge that the students perceive to be essential to student success are directly linked to their statements concerning the actions needed to overcome the "lack of motivation" barrier.

Such actions involve mental analysis on the part of the successful students. According to the participants, the successful student will actively "think about goals" and "push yourself" in order to visualize overcoming motivation barriers. Additionally, participants emphasized the need for successful students to "prioritize" and "do what you need to do first." According to the students, if a student is in a negative home environment that interferes with motivation, it is best to "move in with [a supportive] relative." Also, if the student's family is not a strong proponent of education, the successful student purposefully acts to "not follow in [the] parents' footsteps [if they did not complete school]."

Negative peer pressure—Knowledge and actions.

The students reported that they constantly face external pressures from their peers to join activities that produce negative results. Students who are successful in navigating this barrier possess knowledge that helps them to avoid these pitfalls. "Know not to get involved in gangs," voiced one participant adamantly. All of the groups agreed that the consequences of gang involvement are life altering. The consensus was that successful students "know that gang involvement is not worth it." "Know that peer pressure is powerful," the participants said. Students agreed that gang involvement leads to crime and possible death. Additionally, peer pressure to use illegal drugs is a persistent barrier. Successful students "learn from others who have gone through it [mistake of drug use]," and are aware of the harmful consequences. One student felt that there is negative pressure to become excessively involved in too many extracurricular school activities, to the detriment of a student's ability to keep up with schoolwork. The students indicated that most students on campus avoid this barrier by knowing to "limit yourself to what you can handle." The overall guiding ideology of the students came out in the statement, "education comes first!"

Since the consequences of gang involvement are so serious and sometimes deadly, the participants stated that the safest action concerning gangs is "don't join gangs," and "stay away from gang members." One method of avoiding gangs is to "get involved in sports, ROTC, family, or charity work," which will put students in a better position to be away from gang members. In parallel to avoiding gangs, the participants noted that successful students "don't even start [illegal] drug use" and should "stay away from people who use drugs." The students believed that successful students are able to "spend money on better things [than drugs]." Overall, if a student is having trouble with negative peer pressure, the best thing for a successful student to do is to seek help from a trusted adult. "Get help from teachers," said one participant. The other student participants agreed that being able to avoid powerful negative peer pressure takes deliberate actions on the part of the successful students.

Lack of resources—Knowledge and actions.

Once again, students reported that successful students know and believe that "education is the most important" priority. Even if a student does not feel smart, the participants said, "keep going [don't give up]." Successful students "know to study more" and know to "have mental toughness." That knowledge supports students in building self-confidence, which the participants viewed as an important aspect of overcoming the barrier of lack of mental resources. Also, the participants pointed out that successful students know that failing a class is not a reason to quit trying. "Know that there is summer school [to catch up]" is listed as a resource that successful students can use. With respect to material concerns, successful students "know that [stylish] clothing and other expenses are only temporary [concerns]." The opinion of the students was that successful students believe that education comes first, and other matters can wait. That belief guides the actions of the successful students.

Successful students take actions to overcome their mental challenges. Actively getting "extra help from tutoring," adopting a strong work ethic to "study extra" and "take extra notes" helps students to be successful. "Take summer school, if needed," the participants said. Then, addressing the lack of self-esteem that academically challenged students face, successful students act to "find something you're good at and get involved in it." This action produces positive self-worth and a source of friends that can help with tutoring. Concerning lack of financial resources, the participants noted that students "don't worry about [not having enough money for clothing and other expenses]." If the money issue is truly problematic, the participants stated, then successful students can get a part-time job as long as it does not interfere with school and completing homework.

Systemic failure—Knowledge and actions.

While testing is not new to students in schools, exit testing required to graduate from high school is relatively new and has introduced profound consequences to those students unable to master the exit tests. The students were well aware of this obstacle and provided information about the knowledge that successful students need in order to navigate this barrier to school completion. The participants stated that successful students "know it's [state testing] important" and "take practice tests seriously." Knowing to "pay attention in class" is important as well. Guiding the participants' thinking was the overriding knowledge that successful students are convinced that they "must finish school." Knowing that "you can make more money with a diploma" presents a goal on which successful students can focus. For students who have transferred between schools and have found themselves behind in their work, the participants offered the suggestion that the successful students know to "jump in as fast as you can" and to "make some good friends [good role models]" who can help with tutoring.

The actions of successful students included "take the practice test as often as possible" and studying very hard for these tests. Even though the experience of testing is stressful, the successful students "look forward to the future" and "think about what can happen later on [after graduating]." These actions demonstrate that successful students are not passive about the state-mandated tests, but actively pursue the means needed to pass the exams. Of the students who are new to the school and who are behind due to curriculum inconsistencies between schools, the participants stated, the successful students "[attend] tutoring after school to catch up." Also, it is beneficial to "talk to teachers separately." It is important to "meet new people." According to the students, those actions can help with adjusting to the new school and with obtaining tutoring assistance when needed.

Barrier Taxonomy for Teacher Data

Teacher participants identified barriers to school success along with the knowledge, actions, changes, and problems connected with those barriers. The barriers from the teacher responses were sorted into five categories reflecting the themes of the responses. The five categories of barriers are as follows: (a) low expectations of students for themselves, (b) lack of parental support, (c) negative peer pressure, (d) adjustments, and (e) systemic failure (see Figure 4.2). For each of the barriers identified, teachers revealed the knowledge and actions required by successful students to overcome the barriers. As the student responses also pointed out, the teachers believed that the value placed on education is a major factor in student success. Embedded in the important value assigned to education were personal and institutional knowledge and actions that the teachers believed impacted student success. These included personal characteristics, such as the students being intrinsically motivated and willing to work hard and make sacrifices to reach goals, having a high degree of self-worth, and having resiliency when faced with a setback or failure.

Additionally, teachers connected increased student success with limiting outside work commitments, being serious about school, making good use of school resources, and having friends with positive attitudes. Overall, teachers indicated that successful students understand the value of education and let that value guide thoughts and decisions.

FIGURE 4.2
Barrier Taxonomy for the Teacher Data

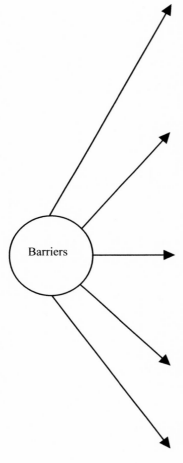

Low Expectations

  •Don't see a future for themselves
  •[Students] don't attach high value to education
  •[Don't] believe in themselves
  •Low self esteem
  •Low school esteem

Lack of Parental Support

  •Low parental educational level [setting poor role model]
  •Parents don't see education as a priority
  •Parents fear children leaving family unit [don't encourage children to seek opportunities]
  •Lack of family structure
  •Bad home life

Negative Peer Pressure

  •Drugs and Alcohol
  •Gangs
  •Negative stigma of being smart

Adjustments
(Mental and Physical)

  •Pregnancy
  •Language barriers
  •Having to have a job
  •Excessive absences

Systemic Failure
  •Skill deficiency
  •Testing

Lack of parental support.

This category elicited a discussion on the effects of family support on the graduation rates at this school. Several teachers stated that one of the barriers to student success is created when "parents don't see education as a priority." Parents who do not make their children come to school and who are not constantly pressuring their children to complete school, teachers said, are not relaying the message of the importance of education. Also, a "low parental educational level" compounds the problem, since the parents are "setting poor role model" examples that their children may choose to follow. The teachers explained that the students may reason, "if my parents did not complete school, then why should I?"

A few teachers voiced the opinion that some parents actually do not want their children to graduate and aspire to attend college because they "fear children leaving [the] family unit." In these cases, the family unit ties are so strong that the parents actually avoid encouragement to complete school out of a desire to keep all of the family intact in one area. The teachers indicated that these parents are caught between two worlds, one of wanting what is educationally best for their children and the other of living in fear that the educational/job opportunities that a high school diploma brings may cause the children to want to leave home permanently, thus breaking the strong family connections.

Negative peer pressure.

Negative peer pressure can have claws that reach out and grab unwary students, dragging them directly away from the path to success. The teachers reported that "drugs and alcohol" as well as "gangs" provided temptations to become involved in harmful activities that could sabotage efforts to obtain a high school diploma. The teachers noted that the students could succeed despite drug or alcohol use, yet those activities usually lead to an ever-increasing spiraling effect away from success, unless intervention is sought. Gang involvement was described by teachers as an enticing draw for students wanting to belong to something. Apparently the previous school year had been one with visible gang involvement on campus. The teachers were pleased that gang-leader and gang-member "round-ups" by the administration during the current school year, combined with lack of tolerance for gang activity, had substantially lowered gang visibility in the school. According to the teachers, administrative action made the school safer and made it less tempting for students to join gangs.

A few teachers mentioned the "negative stigma of being smart" as a barrier. Students who are perceived as smart could become alienated from friends who are not academically adept and success oriented. Other teachers noted that the school tries to counter this negative influence by recognizing student achievement in multiple ways, providing positive feedback for academic success. This is done in hopes that students will be proud of their achievements and make friends who are motivated to be successful. In any case, the teachers perceived a student's friends as an indicator of whether or not the student would be successful.

Adjustments.

This group of barriers contains obstacles that the teachers perceived as major hurdles for some students to overcome, including "having to have a job," "language barriers," "pregnancy," and "excessive absences." Both internal and external forces working on the students generate these barriers. The teachers noted that students with work commitments outside of school were at a disadvantage educationally. Whether the students had to have a job due to family financial circumstances or whether students just wanted spending money, the jobs often worked against their academic achievement due to inadequate time to complete homework or to fatigue. The teachers also noted that, once the students had a foothold in the job market, they often became less interested in schooling and more interested in pursuing the concrete, although low-paying, career path of the individual with no high school diploma.

With respect to language barriers, teachers generally reported that students in their school (mostly Hispanic) did have problems associated with English-as-a-second-language (ESL) issues, even if those students were not receiving ESL services. Getting students to read and understand difficult textbook passages and to write competently were constant struggles, teachers reported. Only two teachers from one group commented that there were no language problems at the school. Since this view was so different from what other teachers had expressed, the teachers reporting no language problems were asked to elaborate on their view. Their comment was that the students are not new immigrants to the United States, and the students do know English but feign not knowing as an excuse to avoid working. There were other teachers within that group who contended that such was not a typical portrayal of the student body.

Teenage pregnancy is not a new barrier to high school students. Pregnant students often have to drop their educational aspirations after the child is born if there are no childcare services available or affordable. Schools have reacted to this barrier in a variety of ways over the years. This particular school is one of only two in its entire multidistrict region to provide onsite daycare for student mothers. The teachers commented that the daycare facility is successful in keeping teen mothers in school, and the daycare's presence lets expectant teen mothers know that they do not have to abandon their education once the child is born.

However, the teachers expressed mixed feelings about the onsite daycare center. On one hand, the teachers felt that the daycare offered opportunity and hope for students who otherwise might not complete their high school education. On the other hand, the teachers perceived that the students no longer worried as much as they should concerning the consequences of trying to parent a child and be a student simultaneously. Several teachers commented that there were students with multiple children attending the high school daycare center. Worried that the accessibility of the daycare actually promotes the barrier of students having children, one teacher emphatically stated, "The girls bring them [children] to school and show them off like trophies!" Even with the daycare center, though, the teachers agreed that being a parent makes school success more difficult. Parenting is difficult and demanding, leaving little time to study. Also, when children are sick, the mothers must keep their children home and cannot attend school. Excessive absences and getting behind in work does become a barrier for student mothers and other students as well.

The barrier of "excessive absences" is sometimes the result of a problem outside of the students' control, such as illness. Other times, excessive absences are a matter of the students' not getting up early enough in the mornings or missing school because of a lack of interest. In either case, the absences create academic problems due to the class information missed. Making up work from absences compounds in difficulty as absences from school increase. The teachers commented that the students can attend absence recovery sessions in order to make up missed school; however, not all students can take advantage of this intervention program.

Systemic failure.

The teachers perceived that "testing" and "skill deficiency" were barriers to school success. Each of these obstacles is the direct result of the school system mechanism failing to provide the essential ingredients for student success. In the case of testing, the teachers were referring to the standardized state testing required for graduation. While many students pass these tests with no problems, the testing does present a barrier to high school completion for students with poor testing skills, limited English language ability, and deficiency in academic subjects. The teachers pointed out that students who enter high school with skill deficiencies are at a tremendous disadvantage and are at risk of not completing high school. The difficulties of "starting out behind" in a subject and "catching up" are overwhelming tasks for some students. After a period of trying, the teachers noted, students perceive they cannot catch up and then give up on school. The teachers were quick to point out that tutoring is available for all students and that many students who need tutoring do not make use of that resource.

The five categories of barriers discussed in the previous section reveal that the teachers perceive many obstacles that must be overcome by the students in order for them to be successful at high school and graduate. In addition to discussing the barriers, the teacher groups also identified the knowledge and actions needed to overcome each of these barriers. This information will be covered in the following section.

Student Knowledge and Action Taxonomies for the Teacher Data

The taxonomies for knowledge and action for the teacher data were created based on the barriers taxonomy already described. The knowledge and actions categories pertaining to each barrier category are shown in Table 4.2.

Low expectations—Knowledge and actions.

According to teachers, the knowledge that students use to overcome the "low expectations" barrier category includes "attach a high value to education." This concept was considered a primary guiding force for success. Additionally, successful students, according to the teachers, know that they must "have short-term and long-term goals," and "with hard work and confidence in their abilities [they] can achieve those goals." For the students to achieve their goals, they must acknowledge the importance of intrinsic motivation and that they must "believe in themselves." In other words, the teachers believed that student success in overcoming low-expectation barriers comes

TABLE 4.2
Knowledge and Action Taxonomies for the Teacher Data

Barrier Category: Low Expectations

Knowledge
- [Students] attach a high value to education
- [Students are] intrinsically motivated
- [Students] believe in themselves
- Have both short term and long term goals
- [Students know] with hard work and confidence in abilities [they] can accomplish their goals
- Make connection between success and enhanced self-esteem
- Know how to build themselves back up again [after failure or disappointment]
- College or military is a path toward success [and must have a diploma]

Actions
- Set goals and follow through
- Develop a plan
- Find their strengths (things they are good at)
- Focus on positive outcomes
- Ask for help
- Associate themselves with other students who have higher expectations
- Spend time with students who have a positive attitude
- Use extracurricular activities as a positive distraction

Barrier Category: Lack of Parental Support

Knowledge
- Know to use other role models
- Know they can rise above parents' achievement [level]
- Know that education is their escape [from a bad home life]
- Understand the fallibility of parental models
- Know that parents will still love him/her [if the child tries to better him/herself through educational opportunities]

Actions
- Believe in themselves
- Develop strengths (guitar, band) [as a distraction]
- Seek out resources available to them (coaches, teachers, mentors, counseling center, ROTC center)
- Use other successful students as role models
- Leave home and go to friends or a safe home

(continued)

TABLE 4.2 (Continued)
Knowledge and Action Taxonomies for the Teacher Data

Barrier Category: Negative Peer Pressure

Knowledge
- Can rise above bad peer pressure
- Understand that there is no future [in gangs]
- [Understand that] jail or death [is the consequence of gang membership]
- Know the consequences of abusing alcohol and drugs
- Understand the possibility of addiction
- Separate partying from school
- Does not care about [the negative] stigma [of being smart]

Actions
- Have meaningful, positive relationships [with other students who are a good influence]
- Associate with other students who have positive influence
- Rely on themselves
- Avoid gangs
- Form new "gangs" (band, honor society)
- Will join religious [or other groups that] don't promote drug and alcohol use
- Encourage each other [against drug and alcohol use]
- Don't wear clothes promoting drugs and alcohol
- Try to reverse the negative stigma of being smart

Barrier Category: Adjustments

Knowledge
- [Having children is] a major roadblock to their goals
- Know that they are not ready for that responsibility [of having children]
- How to budget time
- [How to] prioritize
- Know how to ask for help
- Sacrifice and postpone luxury buying
- Know the importance of being bilingual
- Know many programs and resources [are] available [for overcoming language barrier issues]

Actions
- Avoid relationships [leading to sex]
- Budget time
- Delay [work] until college
- Stop working
- Drop more difficult classes or AP courses [if needed due to having to have a job]
- Come to tutoring [to overcome language barrier]
- Make good use of resources and ESL programs
- Use a Spanish/English dictionary [as needed]

TABLE 4.2 (Continued)
Knowledge and Action Taxonomies for the Teacher Data

Barrier Category: Systemic Failure
Knowledge • Hard work will pay off down the road • Take testing seriously • Know that it [testing] is a learned skill and [they will] get better with practice • [One must] practice long hours to build confidence [in testing]
Actions • Work harder • Apply themselves • Study • Conference with teachers • Take practice tests • Take courses that lead to a postsecondary education

from internal forces that shape a student's thinking about his or her own abilities. Students "make [a] connection between success and enhanced self-esteem," said one teacher. Everyone faces challenges or failures at one point or another. The teachers stated that the successful students know to "build themselves back up again [after failure or disappointment]." Moreover, the low-expectations barriers do not affect the successful students, because they know that there are avenues to success after graduation outside their community, such as through college or the military. The teachers indicated that successful students take these options seriously and act accordingly.

The actions that successful students take to overcome the barriers of low expectations include "setting goals and following through" as well as "developing a plan" of action for success. Actively creating a vision of the future for themselves, successful students use their goals to guide their actions. The teachers indicated that additional actions of successful students are to "find their strengths [what they are good at]" and "focus on positive outcomes." Finding their strengths allows the students to enhance self-esteem through being successful. The teachers commented that it really did not matter what the strength was; it could be anything from playing the guitar well to being good in sports or in any other endeavor. Concentrating on strengths would build self-esteem and improve the students' self-confidence. Indeed, the teachers noted that successful students think about positive rather than negative outcomes. They also know to "ask for help when needed," making good use of available resources, such as tutoring, to enhance their learning.

Of great importance is the wise choice of friends. Successful students take care to "associate themselves with other students with higher expectations." Generating their own peer support system, successful students "spend time with students who have a positive attitude." One method of avoiding negative influences and finding other students with high expectations is for students to "use extracurricular activities as a positive distraction." Activities such as band, athletics, orchestra, theater, and other extracurricular school functions are areas that can lead to creating self-confidence and influential relationships. These actions create the necessary positive influences that not only bolster self-confidence and self-esteem but also provide positive peer role models to enhance goal setting and intrinsic motivation. All of these concepts are based on students acting on the notion that education is valuable to them. Thus, the students' knowledge and actions are aligned with successful completion of high school.

Lack of parental support—Knowledge and actions.

The teachers' comments in this area indicate the belief that many of their students do not come from homes supportive of education. The teachers described some of the students' homes as places where the parents were not well educated, nor very concerned with their children's educational advancement. Moreover, according to teachers, some students struggle with a home life fraught with drugs, alcohol, or even apathetic family members. The knowledge that the successful student needs in order to overcome the barrier of lack of parental support includes "know[ing] to use other role models" such as teachers, coaches, other school personnel, other family members, or even community leaders. Not only do the successful students know that "they can rise above their parents' educational achievement [levels]," but these students also know implicitly that "education is their escape [from a bad home life]."

The teachers also commented that successful students know that parents are not perfect. The students "understand the fallibility of parental models" and choose a different role model, if needed. Successful students know that "parents will still love him/her [if the child tries to better him- or herself through educational opportunities]." Thus, the teachers believe, successful students have a deep understanding of how to select appropriate role models and maintain a vision of success despite lack of parental support.

The teachers reported the actions needed to overcome the barriers in the category of "lack of parental support": Students "believe in themselves" and, in doing so, act to "develop strengths, like guitar, band [as distractions]" to the problems at home. If guidance is not available from home, successful students actively "seek out resources available to them, [including] coaches, teachers, mentors, counseling center, [and] ROTC center." Students can use these resources for advice, help, and positive role models. An interesting side comment made by several of the teachers is that they felt the administration of the school did not want the teachers to offer advice and counseling to the students. Instead, these teachers had understood that teachers should always refer students to the counseling center for guidance. This puzzled the teachers who saw this administrative request as in direct conflict with providing students with accessible, positive guidance and role modeling. If students do not have positive adult role models to choose from, the teachers said, then successful students would "use other successful students as role models."

In considering the most severe cases of lack of parental support, the teachers explained that sometimes the successful students would act to remove themselves from the negative situation. The students would "leave home and go to a friend's home or a safe home" such as that of another relative. Thus, the teachers believe that lack of parental support does not have to be an insurmountable barrier. The knowledge and actions of successful students explain how these students negotiate a home life that does not provide support and stability. However, home life is not the only place where a student might encounter negative influences. School itself can harbor students that wield negative peer pressure in an attempt to influence the beliefs and actions of other students.

Negative peer pressure—Knowledge and actions.

To overcome negative peer pressure, students must know that they "can rise above bad peer pressure." In other words, students need to know that they control their own decisions and are capable of avoiding the negative pressures that might send them on a path leading to failure. The teachers commented that the pressure to join gangs is very real. The successful student "understands that there is no future [in gangs]." Moreover, the successful students realize the catastrophic consequences of being gang members. They understand that "jail or death" are the "consequences of gang membership."

The teachers explained that once a student becomes involved in a gang he or she is usually a permanent, lifelong member.

Use of alcohol and drugs is a negative peer pressure that students face. The successful students know "the consequences of abusing alcohol and drugs" and "understand the possibility of addiction." Therefore, the teachers believe, successful students either do not participate in the parties with drugs and alcohol or limit their participation. These students "don't care about [the negative] stigma [of being smart]" and "separate their partying from school." The teachers feel that, since school is a priority, the successful students do not let social events (parties) ruin or even taint their chances of high school completion. Making good decisions, the wildest parties will be avoided, and the parties that they do attend will not interfere with schoolwork.

Adjustments—Knowledge and actions.

The teachers pointed out how successful students "understand [that having children] is a major roadblock to their goals." Even though daycare is provided for the student mothers, the successful students "know that they are not ready for that responsibility." Additionally, as far as employment goes, the successful students who must work due to the financial needs of their families "know how to budget time," "how to prioritize," and "how to ask for help." The teachers realize that some students must work and go to school, but the successful ones will know time-management techniques to optimize study time. Also, if the student does feel overwhelmed, being able to ask for help offers various resources designed to maintain student success. Tutoring, counseling, and other assistance may provide the elements needed to maintain successful progress in school. The teachers noted that, if the students were working merely to buy luxury items, then that work should be postponed until a later time. In this way, successful students understand the concept of "sacrifice."

Adjustment barriers include the critical role that language plays in student success. The teachers thought that students with multiple language ability should be proud of their achievement and develop it more fully. Successful students, the teachers said, "know the importance of being bilingual." Additionally, if a student is having trouble being competent in English, then the successful student will be one who knows that "many programs and resources [are] available [for overcoming language barrier issues]."

In terms of actions, teachers felt that students should "avoid relationships [leading to sex]." Acting responsibly and not getting caught up in sexual relationships should be a priority among students desiring to complete high school. A second action that teachers suggested for successful students concerns students with work commitments. Working students must actively budget their time, since time must be allotted for classes, work, and homework. If at all possible, the teachers suggested, students should "delay work [until college]" or, if already employed, "stop working" if family finances permit it. Those students in the position of needing to have a job and finding difficulty maintaining good grades should "drop more difficult or advanced placement (AP) courses" that require extensive homework. In the area of language difficulties, the teachers emphasized the importance of students attending tutoring sessions held by teachers, so language problems can be addressed personally. Also, successful students with language barriers can "make good use of resources and ESL programs." One simple yet effective action that successful students can take is to "use a Spanish/English dictionary."

Systemic failure—Knowledge and actions.

"Systemic failure" barriers are obstacles in the paths of many students who have trouble passing the state-mandated exit tests. Such students often have skill deficiencies attributed to failure to acquire foundational skills prior to high school. The teachers identified the knowledge that successful students need to overcome this barrier. Included in this knowledge is the understanding that "hard work will pay off down the road." In other words, successful students know that their dedication to schoolwork will reap big gains at a future date. Teachers stated that successful students also "take testing seriously." Successful students know that whether they graduate from high school or not depends on their performance on the state exit-level tests. The manner in which the successful students approach the test is important as well. These students, according to teachers, "know that it [testing] is a learned skill, and [they will] get better with practice." Since the test scores can improve with practice, successful students know that they "must practice long hours to build confidence" in their testing abilities. Thus, the students who know that testing is an acquired skill that can improve with practice follow through with actions to strengthen their skills and testing abilities. The actions that teachers perceive to be instrumental for successful students include "working harder," "apply[ing] themselves," and "study[ing]." Even students with marginal skills can improve enough to pass classes and graduate if they "conference with teachers" to receive additional help and "take practice tests" to improve their test-taking abilities. Teachers noted that successful students frequently take more challenging courses, including "courses that lead to a postsecondary education." The knowledge that tests are conquerable with hard work and practice, paired with the action of taking practice tests and seeking teacher guidance, creates a picture of a barrier that can be overcome by serious students who desire success. The teachers indicated that any one of their students could be successful and graduate from high school if the knowledge and actions discussed were followed. The barriers identified were not insurmountable by students seeking success.

The teachers indicated that the guiding force behind all decisions and actions of successful students is the strong value placed on education: These students "attach [a] high value to education," and their "hard work will pay off down the road." Moreover, successful students "know that education is their escape." The teachers believe that the students have a better chance of leaving behind a life of low wages and struggling financial existence if the students escape their current surroundings. Thus, education is the path to a better life. According to teachers, successful students strongly value education and let that value direct their knowledge and actions.

Counselor Perspectives

Three counselors (designated here as C-1, C-2, and C-3) reviewed the taxonomic analyses based on the student and teacher data. The counselors tended to agree with students and teachers regarding student success, specifically about the importance of the value students place on education, student involvement as a means of connecting to school, lack of parental communication with teachers, and use of school resources. The three counselors strongly believed that all students could pass despite difficulties, provided they make use of school resources. The counselors directly or indirectly indicated that successful students are motivated and need good friends and role models. This perspective mirrored the views of students and teachers.

C-2 and C-3 disagreed with the students' and teachers' views concerning lack of parental support. While the counselors felt that the parents were supportive of school, students and teachers expressed opinions opposing this view. Students said that parents did not "push them" and "were not behind them," while teachers directly stated that "parents . . . do not see education as a priority" and home life lacks structure. In contrast, C-2 and C-3 adamantly stated that parents do value education, yet do not attend school meetings. Three counselors agreed that the parents lack communication skills when contacting teachers, which is the probable cause of the teachers' believing that parents do not care. Students did not express an opinion in this regard.

In the area of school resources, there was a disagreement among the students, teachers, and counselors. The three counselors agreed that school resources were readily available to those students seeking help. Tutoring from teachers, credit recovery programs, help from counselors and other school personnel, and additional special programs were offered for students willing to participate. The students disagreed, saying the programs were not easy to participate in due to inflexible class scheduling and students' lack of time. The teachers noted that there were many resources available to students to help them succeed in school. However, transportation issues prevented some students from participating. Another area of disagreement concerned the language barrier. While the students, teachers, and C-1 and C-3 agreed that the language barrier was a hindrance to success at this school, C-2 took an opposing view concerning this topic.

The onsite daycare provided by the school for student parents elicited comments from one counselor. C-2 had ambiguous feelings about this resource, which is available to help teen parents. Even though the onsite daycare helped facilitate parenting students to remain in school instead of dropping out, the counselor believed it created an easy "option for girls who might otherwise be more careful." The students and teachers expressed strong opinions opposing the onsite daycare. The students reported that student parents occasionally brought their children to the high school, creating a distraction and implying that students' having children is acceptable. Teachers were even more emphatic about the negative consequences of having onsite daycare. Teachers reported that students brought their children to campus to show them off like a "trophy." Teachers bluntly stated, "do not offer free daycare" because it sends the wrong message to the students.

Perspectives about the adequacy of counseling services were analyzed. There was a discrepancy between the responses of two counselors and the opinions of the students and teachers. Two counselors addressed this topic and believed that there were adequate counseling services offered at the school. C-1 reported 452 assigned students, while C-2 had 270. They stated that the number of counselors was adequate for the number of students. Yet, the students disagreed with the counselors, specifically indicating a need for an additional counselor. Students noted that "access to counselors" was difficult because the "counselors [were] too busy" and "teachers won't let you miss class to see them [counselors]." While the teachers did not directly state the need to hire another counselor, teachers noted the value that good counseling has on student decision making. Teachers did note that the counselors were too busy to see everyone.

Overall, the three counselors agreed that a critical aspect of student success despite barriers is that students must value education. This positive valuation of education helps students to navigate through the barriers they may face, and it also helps to explain why some students are successful despite adversity and challenges in their life experiences.

Administrator Perspectives

Three administrators (designated here as A-1, A-2, and A-3) reviewed the taxonomic analyses of the student and teacher data. The administrators expressed perspectives on student success similar to those of the students and teachers, specifically regarding the importance of valuing education, students being connected to school, students making good decisions in choosing friends and role models, and parental involvement. The three administrators agreed that a strong positive value toward education impacts students' ability to navigate the barriers to high school graduation. This confirmed similar responses from the students, teachers, and counselors. The administrators reiterated the importance of connectedness to school and having good friends and role models for student success. Another area where substantial consensus existed among the adult participants concerns the lack of parent communication with the teachers.

Two of the administrators agreed that the school has a lack of parental support. This echoes the responses of the students and the teachers for this barrier. However, one of the administrators agreed with the two counselors who contended that parents do support the school. Another split relates to the barrier of school resources. One administrator echoed the view of the three counselors and agreed that school resources are available to the students. However, another administrator (A-3) believed that a communication gap contributed to this barrier. Students expressed a similar view, while teachers had opinions that ranged in both directions.

Two of the administrators did not believe that the language barrier was a problem for the school community. The other administrator did not comment on this barrier. The administrators' views contrasted with the opinions of the students, teachers, and two of the counselors, who believed that language barriers did present problems.

All of the counselors, teachers, and students agreed that lack of motivation is a barrier to success on this campus. While two administrators did not comment on this topic, A-3 disagreed on the presence of this barrier. A-3 stated that the students were motivated. However, students and their teachers do not communicate well. A-3 reported that "students are burdened with other responsibilities," but they "do want to be successful."

The topic of onsite daycare was discussed by only one administrator, who believed that it provided a positive contribution to the campus. The administrator did not indicate any problems, as did the students and teachers, who held opposing views. A-1 reported that the onsite daycare helped to keep the school's "high percentage of expectant mothers or student mothers on campus" and attending school.

One administrator stated that the school had an adequate number of counselors. The other two administrators did not cover this barrier. The two counselors who responded to this concern had similar views to this administrator. However, the students believed that there were not enough counselors.

The student, teacher, and counselor data did not identify the barrier of teachers having low expectations of students. Yet, this barrier was identified by one of the administrators, who believed that the teachers with low expectations were generating negative school responses from their students. Low expectations can unravel the connectedness that the students need for success, because they are "perceived by the students as not caring."

In summary, the data obtained from the counselors and administrators provided insight into the perceptions of the school personnel in charge of ensuring student success in the subject school. While not all participants agreed on every barrier, there were significant thematic commonalities, such as the importance that valuing education plays in student success, a student's need to feel connected to school, the inability of parents to communicate with teachers and become actively supportive, and the need for good friends and role models—all of which contribute to student success and high school graduation. The overriding concept related to student success that was stressed by all participants is the value that students place on education. Whether positive or negative, the valuation of education influences students' ability to negotiate the barriers that come between the students and their graduation from high school.

LSSM Concept Model

The study led to an understanding of student success in the context of a high-minority high school. Some core concepts related to student success were identified, including the importance of valuing education, having positive role models, having high self-esteem, avoiding teen parenting, using time-management skills, using school resources for academic assistance, and having a resilient attitude in the face of setbacks. The LSSM created using these concepts illustrates how it is that successful students can overcome the geography of barriers present in the subject school (see Figure 4.3). A key

FIGURE 4.3
LSSM Concept Model of Student Success in a High-Minority High School

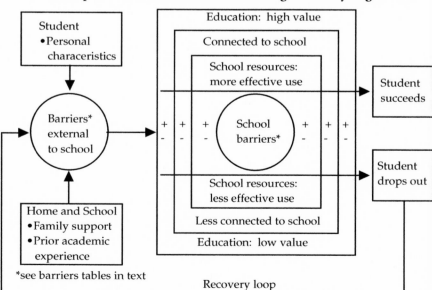

point illustrated by the model is that any means that the school can employ to enhance or facilitate the positive impact of valuing education, students being connected to school, and their effective use of school resources increases the chances of students graduating from high school.

As shown in Figure 4.3, students arrive at the high school with a background that encompasses different degrees of family support, motivation levels, and prior academic experiences. These variables merge to form the context of the student's background. A student's past experiences, including home life, personal motivation, and prior academic experiences, fundamentally shape the abilities and attitudes that the student possesses (Bourdieu, 1998; Coleman, 1988; Croninger & Lee, 2001; Stanton-Salazar, 2004). Thus, the arriving student has a preconditioned sensitivity to education and its value to the student. The student's value of education can range from positive to negative. In other words, students with a positive value of education believe strongly in the importance of education, while students with a negative value of education do not believe that success in school is important to their lives. Successful students are mindful of the importance of education and set goals to attain a high school diploma. Students who can think and act for themselves and set goals prioritizing the importance of education are successful. This, in turn, influences a successful student's motivation, resiliency, and actions when faced with difficulties.

The students and teachers noted that different factors can cause students not to value education. One source of students' negative value toward education can be attributed to the poor decisions students can make in choosing friends and role models. Negative peer pressure, in the form of joining gangs and/or using alcohol and drugs, was mentioned by both students and teachers as a barrier to school success. Such peer pressure negatively impacts a student's valuation of education.

Additionally, the student's valuation of education can be tied to family values and parental role models. The community surrounding the school is a high-minority, low-SES area with limited opportunities for students to access information that would stimulate interest in obtaining jobs different from the role models that surround them. This barrier can be explained by the lack of social capital that the students and families possess (Lucas, 2000; Stanton-Salazar, 2004; Wehlage et al., 1989). Thus, successful students work at building relationships that promote positive influences.

One of the social capital barriers identified by students and teachers is the lack of parental involvement. Israel, Beaulieu, and Hartless (2001) affirm the importance of a supportive family in relation to student success. Lack of parental support for school can diminish the value students place on school, causing students to make minimal efforts to connect with the school or make use of its resources. As shown in the model, being connected to school influences student success. Resilient students can get around this barrier by using role models besides their parents and taking responsibility for their own actions (Grotberg, 2003; Wayman, 2002). Another means of overcoming lack of parental involvement is by choosing friends wisely. Positive peer support can help the student overcome a negative parental situation by providing positive guidance to the student (Reis, Colbert, & Hebert, 2005).

Low self-esteem is a problem that many adolescents face (Woolfolk, 2004). This barrier was identified at this school as well. Freire (2001) and Senge (2000) suggest that the educational system creates low self-esteem or low self-worth among those who cannot adapt to the rigid structure of the school system. Inability to conform to the standards of the school or live up to its expectations creates low self-esteem among some students (Fine, 1991). Students caught between two cultural worlds also can suffer. When the school culture is not sensitive to the students' culture, students can feel disconnected from the school's goals. The available paths to student success are not always accepted by peers, which can cause students to have emotional conflicts and lack self-esteem (Hurd, 2004).

Relationship problems cover a wide variety of issues related to student success. Everything from dysfunctional families and fighting with peers to pregnancy indicates that students can be sidetracked away from success if they are not watchful of relationship barriers. One major roadblock to success was mentioned by all groups of students and teachers—the barrier of students having children and also trying to complete their high school education. Teen pregnancy is a barrier to school success that has long been documented in educational research (Wehlage & Rutter, 1986; Wehlage et al., 1989). Students' having children is perceived to be a problem at this high school even though there is an onsite daycare for student mothers. Both student and teacher groups voiced concern that student parenting is a burden that prevents student success. Yet, the daycare facility may give the impression of acceptance of student parenting as a norm. Because of this misinterpretation, the onsite daycare possibly even encourages students to have children.

Both students and teachers noted that developing time-management skills is essential for students to be able to succeed. Some students have work commitments that can interfere with school. Student and teacher participants expressed the view that trying to maintain a job and be a successful student at the same time adds stress for those students. Unless time is managed efficiently, the students have difficulty completing homework and getting enough rest to be alert in school. Thus, employed students may feel disconnected from school activities and resources, thereby losing focus on the importance of graduating. While some students have jobs because they want extra spending money, other students work out of necessity in order to help their families. In either case, the working students must be able to manage time wisely in order to graduate from high school.

Another barrier that students must overcome in order to be successful is the lack of academic skills. Both students and teachers agreed that academic weakness presents problems for student success, yet these groups also indicated that this barrier is not insurmountable. A variety of school resources are available to assist students with academic problems. Findings by Towns, Cole-Henderson, and Serpell (2001) also show that student success hinges on students, teachers, and administrators working together to provide the resources that students need. Students with knowledge about available help, and the motivation to use it, do seek out various resources to improve academic skills. Moreover, student success depends on students' having social capital in the form of strong positive relationships. These relationships are needed for encouragement and guidance in seeking tutoring or training sessions for students with academic deficiencies.

Resilience is another factor that is important for those students experiencing failure or adversity. Resilient students are able to bounce back and do not let setbacks overwhelm their journey to complete high school. The resilient students achieve success in the face of adversity, or at least bounce back with a positive attitude and self-confidence despite failure (Grotberg, 2003; Tugade & Fredrickson, 2004; Wang & Gordon, 1994; Wayman, 2002). In contrast, nonresilient students become discouraged in the face of failure and give up. Unfortunately, they decide that education is not of value to them, and they leave high school.

As noted in the concept model, a variety of internal and external barriers influence student success. At this particular school, students who value education, feel connected to school, and make good use of school resources are more likely to overcome the barriers that they encounter. In addition, positive self-esteem, a resilient attitude, and good decisions concerning friends and role models are prominent avenues that successful students use to negotiate barriers that might interfere with student success.

The implications for policy and practice are related to issues that potentially thwart student success. Improved communication systems between the school and parents, the counselors and teachers, and the counselors and students are indicated. Additionally, providing ample sources for a variety of good role models could enhance student success. Adolescents sometimes have difficulty envisioning the future and living beyond the moment. Programs to provide students with mentoring, a variety of role models, and training in goal setting would provide valuable focus to direct students toward success. Moreover, the policy of providing onsite daycare may need evaluation by considering the number of students benefited versus the number of students distracted or lured into teen pregnancy due to the daycare's easy access.

Another implication for policy and practice concerns the enormous impact of the value that the school and its personnel place on education and how that value is transmitted to the student population. A school where both students and teachers have high expectations for all is a positive influence on successful high school completion. Staff development is needed to make sure that all of the teachers understand the cultural differences to be expected from their students, as well as the most effective teaching strategies to bring out the best in their students.

Autoethnographic Encounter: The Face of Inequality

Almost any public school teacher in America, when asked, can vividly recount his or her experiences as a first-year teacher. In numerous encounters with teachers over the years, I've yet to find a single teacher who did not experience a steep learning curve, if not a traumatic one, during the first year on the job. For me, it was this experience that profoundly changed my view of the world and led to my orientation toward social justice in education.

I attended high school at Alamo Heights High School in San Antonio and attended Baylor University to obtain my degree and teaching certificate. I returned to San Antonio with a bachelor's degree and teaching certificate

in hand, ready for anything—I thought. I reported to my first teaching position at Cooper Middle School. My work at Cooper was amazingly different
than I expected. The experience provided a tremendous opportunity to connect with and gain experience in a world completely different from what I
had previously encountered. Later on, I discovered that Jonathan Kozol in
Savage Inequalities (1991) used both Cooper Middle School and Alamo
Heights School District as contrasting examples—polar opposites—of
schools with and without resources. The very school in which I obtained my
first teaching position was a school with severe resource limitations (Cooper),
in contrast to the district I was familiar with, which had seemingly unlimited
resources (Alamo Heights). This initial teaching experience shaped my view
of the serious and long-lasting impact of educational policy on the lives of
minorities and disadvantaged families. I was thrown face-first into the world
of disparity. It broke my heart to see smart, disadvantaged students beaten
down with a reality almost void of educational opportunities. Who would
care about these students?

As years of teaching in public schools passed by, I realized that my ability
to make changes there was limited to what I did in my classroom. While I
do believe that teachers make profound differences in individual students'
lives, I felt that I would be in a better position to enact broader change if I
were to work in an administrative position. Thus, I pursued my principal's
certification along with my MA in educational leadership at the University
of Texas at San Antonio (UTSA).

During this time, I was an administrative intern, working as a teacher
and working closely with school administrators. I completed studies encompassing topics such as obstacles of school parental support for ESL families,
characteristics of excellence in school administrators, teacher attitudes
toward inclusion students, and the influence of commercial advertising on
public school students. In each area in which I worked and researched, I
found more evidence that school policy was influenced more profoundly by
work beyond the school administrative level than I had previously thought.
I realized that tools of broad change emanated from effective research, leadership, and published works at a collegiate level. Thus, I began work on my
doctorate in educational leadership so I would have the credentials to build
a reputable career as a university professor.

While completing doctoral requirements, I worked to improve my
knowledge and understanding of the diverse community of learners enrolled

in public schools. I worked with Dr. Raymond Padilla at UTSA, conducting research on the barriers faced by successful, graduating students in high-minority schools in order to divulge the hidden, or not so hidden, hurdles that minority students perceive to be derailing their attempts to succeed in the American school system. I was struck by the concept of illuminating the barriers to success in order to reveal the path to high school completion. Dr. Padilla's research methodology gave voice to the very people most affected by barriers to school success, the students. In a concise, systematic way, the researcher could effectively reach into the heart of the issue. I was influenced by works from giants such as Freire, who provided insight into social justice and raised legitimate questions concerning the disparity of educational opportunity in the public school system.

This became the focus of my research: understanding the intertwined dynamics of school policy and leadership as they meld with student, teacher, administrator, and parent perceptions and actions. Continually, I ask myself, "What can educators do better in order to promote student success?" After all, if a student does not graduate from high school, isn't that an indictment of failure of the entire public school system? I am convinced that U.S. public schools can benefit from more effective leadership and a stronger commitment to excellence. This comment is given even more bite as a national report by Balfanz and Legters (2007) from John Hopkins University characterizes public schools as being "dropout factories." It is true. We as educators can do a better job.

References

Balfanz, R., & Legters, N. (2007, September). *Locating the dropout crisis: Which high schools produce the nation's dropouts? Where are they located? Who attends them?* (Report No. 70). Baltimore, MD: John Hopkins University, Center for Research on the Education of Students Placed at Risk (CRESPAR). Retrieved December 7, 2007, from http://www.csos.jhu.edu/crespar/reports.htm

Bourdieu, P. (1998). *Practical reason.* Stanford, CA: Stanford University.

Coleman, J. S. (1988). Social capital in the creation of human capital. *American Journal of Sociology, 94,* S95–S120.

Croninger, R. G., & Lee, V. (2001). Social capital and dropping out of high school: Benefits to at-risk students of teachers' support and guidance. *Teachers College Record, 103*(4), 548–581.

Fine, M. (1991). *Framing dropouts.* Albany: State University of New York Press.

Freire, P. (2001). *Pedagogy of the oppressed* (M. B. Ramos, Trans.). New York: Continuum. (Original work published 1970)

Grotberg, E. H. (2003). What is resilience? How do you promote it? How do you use it? In E. H. Grotberg (Ed.), *Resilience for today: Gaining strength from adversity* (pp. 1–29). Westport, CT: Praeger.

Hurd, C. A. (2004). "Acting out" and being a "schoolboy": Performance in an ELD classroom. In M. A. Gibson, P. Gandara, & J. P. Koyama (Eds.), *School connections: U.S. Mexican youth, peers, and school achievement* (pp. 63–86). New York: Teachers College Press.

Israel, G. D., Beaulieu, L. J., & Hartless, G. (2001). The influence of family and community social capital on educational achievement. *Rural Sociology, 66*(1), 43–68.

Kozol, J. (1991). *Savage inequalities: Children in America's schools.* New York: Crown.

Lucas, T. (2000). Facilitating the transitions of secondary English language learners: Priorities for principals. *NASSP Bulletin, 84*(619), 2–16.

Reis, S. M., Colbert, R. D., & Hebert, T. P. (2005, Winter). Understanding resilience in diverse, talented students in an urban high school. *Roeper Review, 27*(2), 110–121.

Senge, P. M. (2000). *Schools that learn: A fifth discipline fieldbook for educators, parents, and everyone who cares about education.* New York: Doubleday.

Stanton-Salazar, R. D. (2004). Social capital among working-class minority students. In M. A. Gibson, P. Gandara, & J. P. Koyama (Eds.), *School connections: U.S. Mexican youth, peers, and school achievement* (pp. 18–38). New York: Teachers College Press.

Texas Education Agency. (n.d.). Academic Excellence Indicator System. Retrieved March 6, 2005 form http://www.tea.state.tx.us/perfreport/aeis/index.html

Towns, D. P., Cole-Henderson, B., & Serpell, Z. (2001). The journey to urban school success: Going the extra mile. *The Journal of Negro Education, 70*(1/2), 4–18.

Tugade, M. M., & Fredrickson, B. L. (2004). Resilient individuals use positive emotions to bounce back from negative emotional experiences. *Journal of Personality and Social Psychology, 86*(2), 320–333.

Wang, M. C., & Gordon, E. W. (1994). *Educational resilience in inner-city America.* Hillsdale, NJ: Erlbaum.

Wayman, J. C. (2002). The utility of educational resilience for studying degree attainment in school dropouts. *The Journal of Educational Research, 95*(3), 167–178.

Wehlage, G. G., & Rutter, R. A. (1986, Spring). Dropping out: How much do schools contribute to the problem? *Teachers College Record, 87*(3), 374–392.

Wehlage, G. G., Rutter, R. A., Smith, G. A., Lesko, N., & Fernandez, R. R. (1989). *Reducing the risk: Schools as communities of support.* Philadelphia: Falmer.

Woolfolk, A. (2004). *Educational psychology* (9th ed.). Boston: Pearson Education.

5

STUDENT SUCCESS IN A COMMUNITY COLLEGE

Ralph Mario Wirth

E ffective educational practice is part of the constellation of social
forces that can positively shape the future of a nation's citizenry. According to the U.S. Secretary of Education's Commission on the Future of Higher Education, "postsecondary institutions have accomplished
much of which they and the nation can be proud" (Commission, 2006, p.
ix). However, the Commission also stated that despite past achievements
"U.S. higher education needs to improve in dramatic ways" (p. ix). The
Commission's first recommendation for the improvement of higher education focuses on student success, recommending that "the U.S. commit to
an unprecedented effort to expand higher education access and success by
improving student preparation and persistence, addressing nonacademic
barriers and providing significant increases in aid to low-income students"
(p. 17).

Along the same lines, recent studies related to access include warnings
of a decrease in postsecondary educational opportunity (Couturier, 2006)
and emphasize the need to support student participation before and during
postsecondary education (Adelman, 2007). This chapter focuses on the experiences of successful students in navigating campus barriers at a community
college in south Texas. The Expertise Model of Student Success served as the
framework for creating a local model of student success for the subject campus. In addition, an implementation model for student services was created
based on EMSS. The implementation model is in line with Tinto's (2006)
call for effective institutional action.

Barriers to Student Success at Community Colleges

A review of research conducted on community colleges suggests that Padilla and Pavel (1986) were likely the first to study the success of community college students. Their decision to study Hispanic students on two campuses, Phoenix College and Mesa Community College, in the Maricopa County Community College District (MCCCD) was "motivated from the desire to move ahead with positive actions and to achieve better educational results" (Padilla & Pavel, 1986, p. 5). As a result of their research at MCCCD, Padilla and Pavel were able to classify in specific detail the barriers to success for Hispanic community college students. Among these barriers were those related to (a) the institution or institutional processes, (b) classroom functions and instruction, (c) a student's environment outside the campus, (d) financial matters, and (e) a student's personal characteristics.

Utilizing a number of focus groups, Rendón (1993) conducted a study of 49 at-risk community college students. She concluded that invalidation constituted the major barrier to successful learning. Furthermore, she reported that student interaction with either noncaring faculty or those faculty who discount student life experiences was a key driver of this barrier. Rendón also found that the discrediting of the collegiate nature of community colleges by a student's family and friends had a similar effect. She provided a list of characteristics of students whose campus involvement is problematic and consequently have difficulty navigating campus life. These characteristics include immaturity, fearfulness, academic underpreparation, self-centeredness or introversion, a lack of self-initiative, the absence of clear goals, and self-doubt or a failure to ask the right questions.

Hagedorn, Perrakis, and Maxwell (2004) used data collected in focus groups of students, faculty, and administrators at nine community colleges in Los Angeles to explore obstacles to student success. Their research was part of the federally funded Transfer and Retention of Urban Community College Students (TRUCCS) project. The authors found 10 areas that hindered student success: poor and inconsistent counseling, lack of transfer support, inadequate career counseling, red tape, disconnectedness from faculty and campus culture, insufficient technological resources, lack of mathematics and basic English competencies, a lack of support by part-time faculty, inadequate facilities for studying and parking, and poor or nonexistent course advising.

In her study of coping styles among 111 Hispanic students enrolled in liberal arts classes in a community college in Southern California, LeSure-Lester (2003) found that "the key factors determining college persistence decisions for Latino students are academic development, faculty concern, and faculty interest in students" (p. 18). Similarly, based on his experiences as assistant dean of academic affairs at New Jersey's Mercer County Community College, Bolge (1994a) provided a list of access barriers and described a number of barrier-breaking programs implemented at Mercer. According to Bolge, barriers at Mercer included personal, socio-economic, socio-cultural, socio-educational, and institutional factors, as well as barriers arising from federal and state regulations. Bolge (1994b) also conducted an exploratory study involving 57 remedial instructors to better understand their perceptions of the barriers to success faced by remedial students. He found that instructors identified seven significant barriers: insufficient time to study, competing employment demands, countervailing family and domestic demands, lack of childcare, car problems, limited funds, and vague career plans. Of these seven, the surveyed faculty regarded the first four as the most significant.

One of the reports of Manpower Demonstration Research Corporation's (MDRC) project, Opening Doors to Earning Credentials, was conducted by Jobs of the Future researchers with an unidentified number of focus groups consisting of low-income community college students. The purpose of the Opening Doors project, which was funded by the Lumina Foundation and seven other organizations, was to explore program redesign strategies that would enhance the success of low-income community college students (Kazis & Liebowitz, 2003). This study found that time constraints—due to combined family, work, and school responsibilities—as well as basic skills deficiencies were major obstacles to success.

A few studies address barriers related to transfer students. In their literature review, Lynch, Harnish, and Brown (1994) identified several barriers to transferring credit courses from community and technical colleges to senior colleges and universities. Among these barriers were faculty attitudes, the lack of an institutional commitment to access, campus inaccessibility, financial challenges, and structural constraints (specialized two-year versus general four-year institutions). In a presentation at the New Mexico Institute, Rendón (1995) divided transfer barriers into three groups: institutional barriers, cultural barriers, and out-of-class barriers. According to Rendón, institutional barriers are related to poor counseling, college costs, lack of articulation, and channeling of students into vocational-technical tracks. Among Hispanic students in particular, Rendón identified unsupportive families and fear of leaving home as principal out-of-class barriers. Furthermore, she held that a lack of role models, the absence of encouragement, and discouraging peer pressure were sources of out-of-class barriers. Myhre (1998) explored the transfer function at City College of San Francisco, including barriers to transfer, by interviewing 30 faculty, 15 administrators, and 60 students. She identified bureaucratic hurdles, racism, and misinformation from faculty as the main barriers to transfer.

A study by Webb (1989) was based on the evaluation of 36,603 records of full-time and part-time students from three campuses in the Los Angeles Community College District. His model shows four factors having a primary effect on degree persistence—academic achievement in high school, external environment, goal commitment, and student–college fit expected by students—while background characteristics such as academic intent and academic self-confidence have secondary effects in his model. Social integration was shown to have only possible effects, while academic integration was viewed as having a secondary effect on degree persistence, depending on background, external environment, and expected fit. Compared to Tinto's (1987) and Bean and Metzner's (1985) models, Webb relegated social integration to a minor role, and he eliminated psychological outcomes while emphasizing the external environment and academic self-confidence—the latter being a significant factor also for Rendón's validation model.

Stahl and Pavel (1992) conducted a survey of 785 urban community college students enrolled in the beginning courses of reading, English, and mathematics. Assessing Bean and Metzner's (1985) model, the researchers concluded, "the Bean and Metzner model was an extremely weak-fitting model for the empirical data of this study" (Stahl & Pavel, 1992, p. 19). In order to represent their data well, they developed a conceptual model for retention of community college students consisting of six constructs: academic identity (e.g., educational goals), academic commitment (e.g., study habits), academic interference (e.g., employment), educational benefits (e.g., transfer intent), satisfaction (e.g., advisement), and academic achievement (e.g., semester GPA). A decade later, in their mixed-methods study of student life and course completion, Hagedorn, Moon, Maxwell, and Pickett

(2002) posited that "course completion is the appropriate way to conceptual-ize retention within a community college sample" (p. 2). They administered a 47-item questionnaire developed for the Transfer TRUCCS project to a sample of 4,433 students in the Los Angeles Community College District (LACCD). Based on their findings, the researchers developed a community college model of student life and retention. They used the typology proposed by Benjamin (1994) in his quality-of-student-life model, which views student satisfaction as being at the core of the student's interactions with the institu-tional environment. Hagedorn et al.'s (2002) constructs included variables such as (1) conditioning (i.e., demographics), (2) independent (e.g., obsta-cles), (3) mediating (e.g., beliefs), and (4) the dependent variable (course completion).

Hagedorn et al. (2002) extrapolated several significant points from their model, including the role of student life as predictor of course completion, the importance of English proficiency as a predictor of student life as well as course completion, and their counterintuitive finding of obstacles as positive predictors of course completion. According to the authors, the latter indi-cates that "while obstacles create roadblocks to student life, urban commu-nity college students can be resilient and thus not significantly less likely to complete their courses" (p. 13) as compared to students in other institutions of higher education. The importance of obstacles or barriers with respect to student success is consistent with research conducted earlier (e.g., Padilla & Pavel, 1986; Padilla, Treviño, Gonzalez, & Treviño, 1997). In both of these studies the authors focused on student success by retrieving information about how students successfully navigate a specific campus. They suggested that such information can be integrated into various student support ser-vices, such as student advising and orientation, that can result in enhanced student success.

Miller, Pope, and Steinmann (2005) also support the role of student ser-vices in "understanding student concerns, needs, and approaches to success" (p. 64). In their study, they profiled challenges and stressors faced by com-munity college students in two urban, two suburban, and two rural commu-nity colleges in a nonspecified geographical area. Out of a survey sample of 300 students in introductory mathematics courses, 91 percent responded. The data analysis revealed three predominant challenges: academic success, balancing academic and social life, and college costs. Major challenges included thinking about the future, finding career and personal direction, and making lifestyle choices. On the other hand, students in this study were least challenged by finding transportation to campus, making choices about health issues, and finding spiritual direction. Major response strategies by students included consulting with a family member and using college academic advising along with financial aid services. Clearly, many of these studies reflect a shift to the study of student success and how to achieve it.

Site

Hill Country Community College (HCCC, pseudonym) enrolls approximately 8,000 students. According to the basic classifications of the Carnegie Foundation for the Advancement of Teaching, HCCC is an associate-degree, public, urban-serving multicampus (Hardy & Katsinas, 2006). HCCC's latest statistics show that the majority of students were female (58 percent) and ethnically either White (45 percent) or Hispanic (46 percent), and 58 percent of students attended classes on a part-time basis. Forty percent were academically disadvantaged, and 69 percent were economically disadvantaged. In the fall of 2003, 34 percent of surveyed students reported full-time employment, whereas 32 percent reported part-time employment. Almost 10 percent reported that they were single parents.

Following Patton (1990), a purposeful sample was selected for this study for two reasons: It captures major variations within a relatively small sample, and common themes are more likely to emerge during data analysis. Students in the sample had to meet the following criteria: (1) They matched the ethnic and gender percentages of the general student population, (2) they were enrolled for a minimum of 12 hours, (3) they were no more than 24 years old, and (4) they were in their second year at the college pursuing one of the college's three associate degrees (Adelman, 2006). The sampling excluded those students seeking certificates, even though they represent a significant percentage of all credential completers, but with less continuous, long-term campus presence. Four focus groups with a total of 22 student participants were assumed to be sufficiently representative to achieve breadth while still enabling the researcher to attain depth within set boundaries (Patton, 1990; Miles & Huberman, 1994). The participants in the focus groups mirrored the ethnic and gender composition of the college student body.

The second sample of participants consisted of student advisors with whom individual interviews were conducted. Student advisors were identified because it has been suggested that the quality of their contact with students contributes to student success (Richardson & Skinner, 1990). The criteria for selecting six advisors were length of service, regular and frequent student contact, understanding of student challenges, and comparability to the student sample in terms of ethnic and gender composition.

The data were analyzed according to the EMSS framework (see chapter 2) to generate a local student success model (both as a taxonomic model and as a concept model). The results of the analysis are presented below.

The Taxonomic LSSM

Tables 5.1 through 5.6 present the taxonomy of barriers based on the student data. Barriers represent aspects of challenges to individual student persistence and success related to the target campus. However, a number of off-campus obstacles, such as personal barriers, also impact on-campus success. Barriers were grouped into six categories that were inductively derived.

TABLE 5.1
Personal Barriers

1.0	Health problems (physical/emotional)
1.1	Keeping mental sanity
1.2	Finding balance w/social life
1.3	Lack of time management skills
1.4	Scheduling (job and college)
1.5	Family and children (responsibilities)
1.6	Education interferes with family life
1.7	Lack of support by family and friends
1.8	Transportation

TABLE 5.2
Financial Barriers

2.0	Job
2.1	Unemployment
2.2	Student loans

TABLE 5.3
Coursework Barriers

3.0	Lack of instructor support
3.1	Lack of motivation by instructors
3.2	Level of instruction doesn't match expectations
3.3	Short notice of assignments
3.4	Delayed online posting of grades
3.5	Mandatory out-of-class group work
3.6	Finding out the importance of each class
3.7	Limited online access to submit assignments online
3.8	Negative student behavior in class
3.9	Fellow students lacking skills and motivation (group work)

TABLE 5.4
Learning Barriers

4.0	Being undecided (major)
4.1	Discipline (staying focused)
4.2	Lack of attention span
4.3	Hard to concentrate
4.4	Lack of study habits
4.5	Lack of study groups
4.6	Lack of note taking skills
4.7	Lack of communication skills
4.8	Problems with the English language
4.9	Lack of computer literacy
4.10	Lack of personal computers
4.11	Making time for study

1. Personal barriers as related to the individual student's health, family, social life, and abilities.
2. Financial barriers as related to a student's employment status, funding (especially with respect to reliance on loans), and expenses.
3. Coursework barriers as related to classroom issues and instructors.
4. Learning barriers as related to academic preparedness and the skills needed to navigate the institution and successfully engage in coursework.
5. Institutional barriers as related to institutional facilities, policies, and rules relevant to academic issues (excluding support services).
6. Student support barriers as related to institutional services.

TABLE 5.5
Institutional Barriers

5.0	Confusing to get into school (college)
5.1	Lack of information on extracurricular activities
5.2	Restrictions for students advertising student activities
5.3	Lack of recreation facilities
5.4	Lack of social life on campus
5.5	Insufficient study areas
5.6	Computer system crashes
5.7	Lack of computers on campus
5.8	Limited access to available computers
5.9	Scheduling of many events not student friendly
5.10	Limited library hours
5.11	College is not open on Sundays
5.12	Parking

TABLE 5.6
Student Support Barriers

6.0	Advisors are not on the same page
6.1	No designated advisors
6.2	Long waits for access to advisor
6.3	Insufficient guidance regarding programs of study
6.4	Wrong information on degree plans
6.5	Insufficient guidance regarding career focus
6.6	Lack of guidance for the undecided
6.7	Lack of support for student activities
6.8	Lack of communication within student services
6.9	Limited access to online registration

Each barrier category is followed by the exemplars for that category. Among the 59 barriers identified by the students in the regular focus groups, institutional barriers were the most frequently noted (13), followed by those related to learning (12), coursework (10), student support (10), and personal (9) and financial issues (5).

Heuristic knowledge refers to the nature of student expertise, and it composes part of the student's compiled knowledge (see chapter 2). This knowledge helps students to identify and overcome barriers. The more heuristic knowledge a student possesses prior to college admission and the faster a student acquires new heuristic knowledge after enrollment, the more skillful he or she will be in overcoming barriers. The corpus of heuristic knowledge was grouped into five categories that were inductively derived:

1. Experiential knowledge (knowing situations and drawing conclusions from experiences)
2. Knowledge about study and skills
3. Procedural knowledge (for performing a task)
4. Relational and comparative knowledge (recognizing relationships between phenomena)
5. Motivational knowledge (to direct behavior)

Tables 5.7 through 5.11 show the categories of heuristic knowledge based on the student data.

Tables 5.12 through 5.15 present the taxonomy of actions based on the student data. Student actions constitute the pivotal step toward overcoming barriers. It is the individual student's possession of conative competence (i.e., will, energy, and action) that often distinguishes successful students from less successful students. Based on their knowledge of identified barriers, successful students follow through with actions to overcome barriers in various ways. Student actions were grouped into four categories that were inductively derived:

1. Strategic actions as they pertain to planning and achieving
2. Pragmatic actions as they pertain to solving problems in a practical manner
3. Persuasive actions as they pertain to inducing action or change of attitude in others
4. Supportive actions as they pertain to furnishing assistance or ensuring inclusion

Each category of actions is followed by the exemplars for that category.

The LSSM as a Concept Model

The LSSM as a concept model (see Figure 5.1) describes the relationship between barriers to student success, the corpus of heuristic knowledge, and the action repertoire of successful students at HCCC. The model focuses on the

TABLE 5.7
Experiential Knowledge

Experiential Knowledge
Subcategory 1: Self-understanding
7.0   We're here for ourselves
7.1   More education means a better life
7.2   Activities help expand our minds
7.3   There are limitations on social life
7.4   Know your limitations
7.5   The change has to come from within to say, "I need to have more discipline"
7.6   If you don't have it, you fail (discipline)
7.7   Know that if you don't study you fail
7.8   Focus depends on interest in particular class
7.9   Know you need to take classes seriously
7.10 Need more awareness, basically (at college)
7.11 If they don't offer the classes . . . it makes it a lot harder
7.12 If I can find reasons that it's important, then I am interested in it (course)
7.13 Know all that is out there that fits you best
Subcategory 2: Alienation
7.14 To most college means just go there to listen, then go back (home/to work)
7.15 Most are just here to go to class and go home
7.16 It's a lot like high school here . . . you're just not here all day
7.17 To many it's just a community college
7.18 Classroom behavior often atrocious (students)
Subcategory 3: Financial Issues
7.19 Financial help is available (through HCCC)
7.20 There is injustice regarding student loans
7.21 Know rules and qualifications for loans
7.22 There are lots of special cases (for financial aid)
7.23 Students have different sets of problems (loan/aid applicants)
7.24 Not enough money to go to school
7.25 No support from friends or at home makes it harder
Subcategory 4: Employment
7.26 Hard to find jobs in neighborhoods
7.27 Hard to find jobs that coincide with school

TABLE 5.7 (Continued)

Experiential Knowledge
Subcategory 5: Advising and Student Support
7.28 Advisors have information resources
7.29 Advisors have *their* agenda for me, not my agenda
7.30 Assigned advisor would be easier
7.31 One can make arrangements to see same advisor
7.32 Some really know what they're doing, and a lot don't (advisors)
7.33 A lot (of advisors) don't know what they are doing
7.34 Aware of lack of information on schedules (advisors)
7.35 Lack of information on program choices (advisors)
7.36 Many students lack awareness of career and personal counseling services
7.37 Nobody knows that she's here (career counselor)
7.38 We have the career center but it is kind of hidden
Subcategory 6: Institutional Issues
7.39 Know the territory regarding parking
7.40 People come at certain times during the day (parking)
7.41 Parking close to all classes [is] most convenient
7.42 Nearly every class requires group work
7.44 Almost everything is on-line
7.45 It crashes all the time (PC system)
7.46 We've grown three times as much as we were meant to hold

expertise developed by those students who successfully navigate the barriers on the HCCC campus. As shown in the model, students already possess some heuristic and academic knowledge before entering HCCC. After arriving on campus, students encounter barriers, as shown in Tables 5.1 through 5.6. Prior heuristic knowledge combined with heuristic knowledge newly acquired on campus composes student expertise, which can lead to taking appropriate actions to overcome these barriers.

The "Barriers" box in the model shows the empirically determined categories of barriers that students encounter. If students do not manage to overcome these barriers, they may need to acquire more heuristic knowledge, as indicated in the center of the model by the box labeled "Acquire more heuristic knowledge." On the other hand, if students take ineffective actions, as represented by the box so labeled, they may try to gain more heuristic knowledge, take different actions, or possibly decide to withdraw.

The bottom half of the model shows the acquisition of academic knowledge. Prior to entering HCCC, students already possess a certain amount

TABLE 5.8
Knowledge About Study and Skills

Knowledge About Study and Skills
Subcategory 1: Improvement of Learning and Skills 8.0   Know what best fits you (classes) 8.1   Know which courses to take 8.1   There are courses to overcome language problems 8.2   Know about Student Success Seminars 8.3   Know you can improve study skills 8.4   Know you need communication skills 8.5   Know that you need to be computer literate
Subcategory 2: Times and Places of Study 8.6   Sunday is study day 8.7   Need to study in the PC Lab 8.8   Need to study in library 8.9   Need to study in study areas 8.10 Need a place to study before and after class
Subcategory 3: Assignments 8.11 Too much homework simultaneously 8.12 Time issues when notice on assignments is too short 8.13 Too much homework in mid-week 8.14 Weekend assignments are best
Subcategory 4: Group Work 8.15 Not all students work at same pace 8.16 Not all students participate in group work 8.17 Stuck with a group that doesn't do anything 8.18 Not everybody does assignments in group work 8.19 Many group projects could be done individually 8.20 A lot of times instructors are not flexible (group work)

of academic knowledge. When students have acquired sufficient academic knowledge on campus according to HCCC's academic standards, they will achieve success. While their academic knowledge is insufficient, they either acquire additional academic knowledge (facing the barriers to its acquisition) or they may decide to leave HCCC. The top and bottom arrows indicate that the development of student expertise occurs over time.

The LSSM concept model explains two parallel student success processes. In the nonacademic sphere, the sooner that students starting at HCCC are able to identify barriers associated with college attendance, the sooner

TABLE 5.9
Procedural Knowledge

Procedural Knowledge
Subcategory 1: Inquiries 9.0 Need to know what to ask 9.1 Know what to ask 9.2 Know how to ask 9.3 It's possible to ask where things are 9.4 Know what you're doing to get right help
Subcategory 2: Institutional Issues 9.5 Enrolling and knowing guidelines is confusing 9.6 Hard to get our stuff out (student PR work)

TABLE 5.10
Relational and Comparative Knowledge

Relational and Comparative Knowledge
Subcategory 1: Balance 10.0 Know your availability to work and school 10.1 Physical health promotes both mental and emotional health 10.2 Time management, study skills, and social life have to go hand in hand
Subcategory 2: Institutional 10.3 Instructors lack understanding of students' lives outside of school 10.4 Know lack of information on colleges by high schools
Subcategory 3: Coursework 10.5 Other students affect personal grades (group work) 10.6 Communication skills important for group work 10.7 Time conflicts in out-of-class group work 10.8 Peer relations make class more enjoyable
Subcategory 4: Finances 10.9 Know book/food prices elsewhere 10.10 Items twice as expensive as in high school (food/books)

they will be able to acquire sufficient heuristic knowledge about those barriers to become expert students. Expert students then use their conative capacity to turn their knowledge into actions to overcome barriers. That is, they possess and apply motivational and volitional energy to transform knowledge into action. In the academic sphere, when students acquire sufficient academic knowledge to meet program requirements, they will achieve

TABLE 5.11
Motivational Knowledge

Motivational Knowledge
Subcategory 1: Individual
11.0   Time for leisure needed
11.1   Need rest
11.2   Know you need to stay focused
11.3   Interest in course increases with seeing its importance/relevance
11.4   Need reasons that this class is important
11.5   You need those extra things to keep you motivated in school (extracurricular)
Subcategory 2: Social
11.6   Students need to be involved to help others
11.7   More activities attract participation [of students] in a lot of other things
11.8   Having friends makes a class so much more enjoyable
11.9   Making friends at work or in class is helpful
11.10 Friends on campus are important

academic success. In both cases, mechanisms are in place to make up for insufficient heuristic knowledge, ineffective actions, and lack of academic knowledge. Failure to use these mechanisms may lead to withdrawal from college.

Analysis of the advisor data showed that the advisors' frequent agreement with student-derived models seemed to reflect their interaction with engaged students, while advisor comments on barriers seemed to refer to their experiences with behaviors displayed by less engaged students. The advisors acknowledged the persistent, proactive, and self-motivating tendencies displayed by engaged students. They also pointed out their numerous ways of reaching out to all students, which included brochures, the HCCC website, their extended business hours, and more.

However, to their own regret, the advisors' goal of rendering the advising process effective for the majority of students has not yet been reached. Obstacles that advisors encounter include a lack of student engagement, as well as a lack of student self-determination to act according to their own—and sometimes insufficient—heuristic knowledge to overcome barriers. Obstacles also may include the advisors' lack of specific knowledge regarding student barriers and student knowledge about barriers. This is commonly true for situations with high student–advisor ratios and little chance for intrusive advising.

TABLE 5.12
Strategic Actions

Strategic Actions
Subcategory 1: College, Work, and Family
12.0   Base school around family and children
12.1   Work around your schedule
12.2   Flex your own schedule (work/classes/family)
Subcategory 2: Study and Learning
12.3   Learn skills to make the most of time
12.4   Set time aside for your studying for your score
12.5   Develop better study habits
12.6   Write a list of things important to studying
12.7   Set up own study group
12.8   Take ESL classes
12.9   Attend student development success seminar
12.10 Attend classes to become computer literate
Subcategory 3: Course Selection
12.11 Take assessment test to find out your program fit
12.12 Find out yourself what classes to take
12.13 If you waited in the right line, you'd find out about it (right classes)
12.14 Make lists of classes and their importance
12.15 Write down reasons that this class is important
Subcategory 4: Advising
12.16 Request same advisor
12.17 See advisor several times

An Implementation LSSM for HCCC

To enhance student advising and student services, an implementation LSSM was developed, as shown in Figure 5.2. The implementation LSSM may provide HCCC with the opportunity to promote an environment of high-level student engagement as well as to monitor the acquisition of compiled knowledge by students. Student services play a key role in this model (Komives & Woodard, Jr., 2003).

Following the theory and methods underlying LSSM (see chapter 2), the purpose of the implementation model is to serve as a data-driven tool for improving student services in a constant and consistent manner at HCCC. With its focus on heuristic knowledge, the implementation LSSM will complement existing institutional ways of assisting students. As shown in Figure 5.2, the implementation LSSM can improve student services because it

TABLE 5.13
Pragmatic Actions

Pragmatic Actions
Subcategory 1: Family and Work
13.0   Get babysitter
13.1   Make arrangements (with family)
13.2   Negotiate time issues with employer
13.3   Talk to co-workers about schedule
13.4   Settle it, get a mediator or move out (conflicts with parents)
Subcategory 2: Finances
13.5   I have to go to my parents (financial help)
13.6   Borrow money
13.7   Apply for financial aid/scholarship
13.8   Look for jobs (yourself)
13.9   Ask family about job availabilities
13.10 Use Internet job search
13.11 Bring your own food (cafeteria prices)
13.12 Buy online/in other bookstores
Subcategory 3: Studying
13.13 Find study area that is less crowded
13.14 I just go to work when it's really quiet and do it (study)
13.15 I go to Barnes & Nobles (study)
Subcategory 4: Transportation and Parking
13.16 Take distance education (to avoid parking issues)
13.17 Get a car
13.18 Get into a car pool
13.19 Take bus
13.20 Use shuttle
13.21 Get a bike
13.22 Be ready to walk
13.23 Park further away
13.24 Time yourself
13.25 Come earlier
Subcategory 5: Instructors and Advisors
13.26 Inform instructor about work schedule
13.27 Inform your teacher about scheduling conflicts (out-of-class group work)
13.28 Talk to student advisor

TABLE 5.14
Persuasive Actions

Persuasive Actions
Subcategory 1: Instructors and Group Work
14.0   Ask instructor to drop non-participating members in group work
14.1   Make instructor aware of time conflicts related to out-of-class group work
14.2   Ask instructor for options regarding group work
14.3   Ask instructor to assign homework over weekends
Subcategory 2: Instructors' Attitude
14.4   Let professors know they need more understanding (support)
14.5   Ask instructor to post grades in due time

TABLE 5.15
Supportive Actions

Supportive Actions
15.0   Talk to fellow students and make friends
15.1   You ought to support other students
15.2   Let us do a lot more for the students
15.3   We need to work on outreach
15.4   Encourage fellow students' participation (group work)

- Places the focus on the students' heuristic knowledge. Student services professionals become more aware of enhancing each student's heuristic knowledge as quickly and comprehensively as possible.
- Provides methods for periodic qualitative surveys using the unfolding matrix that produce data to drive student services as student needs change.
- Can be applied to the general student population or to subpopulations to meet both general and particular student needs.
- Integrates student and staff perspectives into institutional practices to enhance student success.

The implementation model is divided into three aspects: (1) the basis for student service, (2) interactions and service delivery, and (3) outcomes. The model shows the addition of the EMSS framework and the taxonomic LSSM to the institution's mission and policies as the basis for student services. The taxonomic LSSM provides HCCC student services with information about

FIGURE 5.1
LSSM as a Concept Model of Student Success at HCCC

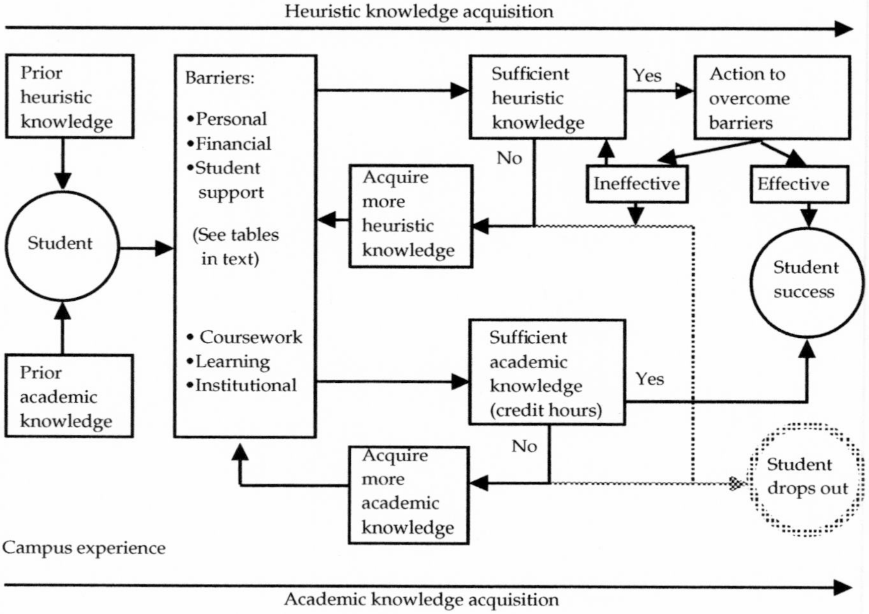

Heuristic knowledge acquisition

Prior heuristic knowledge

Barriers:
- Personal
- Financial
- Student support

(See tables in text)

- Coursework
- Learning
- Institutional

Student

Prior academic knowledge

Sufficient heuristic knowledge — Yes → Action to overcome barriers

No

Acquire more heuristic knowledge

Ineffective   Effective

Student success

Sufficient academic knowledge (credit hours) — Yes

No

Acquire more academic knowledge

Student drops out

Campus experience

Academic knowledge acquisition

relevant and current barriers to student success on campus. On the basis of staff–student dialogue, the barriers to student success can be addressed through appropriate student services. Service delivery consists of advising, financial aid, career and personal counseling, student assessment and testing, and so on. Moreover, service delivery contains the element of *monitoring* by student affairs professionals to ensure that students are indeed overcoming the barriers that they encounter. If a barrier is overcome, the student continues with his or her endeavors at HCCC. If a barrier is not overcome, the student may decide to reenter into a staff–student dialogue to obtain additional assistance, or perhaps opt to leave the institution.

Implications of the Study

Embedding student and staff perspectives into existing institutional assessment practices through regular qualitative surveys may contribute to the collaborative culture currently guiding HCCC. Continuing inclusion of students also may attract less engaged students to regular advising and other

FIGURE 5.2
Implementation LSSM for HCCC

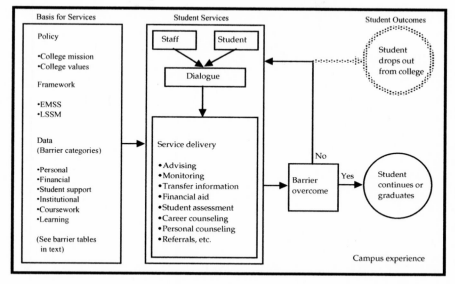

services as well as concretely demonstrate HCCC's student-centeredness with its emphasis on learning. This approach is consistent with Tinto's (2002) concept of social support within an educational community and "the capacity of institutions to establish educational communities that involve all students as equal members" (p. 4). Effective institutional leaders adhering to an integrated leadership model representing elements of creative and transformational leadership theory should take into account that this approach includes listening to student needs and suggestions for change within an institution. EMSS provides a method for systematically listening to students and other stakeholders on campus.

Practice

According to a recent Lumina Foundation report (Dowd, 2005) emphasizing the role of practitioners in data-based benchmarking, the involvement of student services professionals in the deployment of the implementation LSSM is essential for effective student services. EMSS requires student services professionals—and advisors in particular—to remain knowledgeable at all times about the barriers that students face on their campus. EMSS also views advisors and other staff persons as promoters of student expertise according to the social dynamics and academic requirements specific to their campus. If barriers are addressed then services are likely to improve.

Future Research

Three implications for future research stand out: (1) the need to develop an LSSM for each community college, (2) the need to generalize across the various LSSMs, and (3) the need to develop a pedagogy of heuristic knowledge so that student expertise can be enhanced across the board.

Each educational setting is unique, and so are its ways of changing. Consequently, for the purpose of institutional improvement, developing both local models of student success and local implementation models for student services needs to be part of the agenda for institutional research in each local educational setting. This research may be extended *within* an individual community college to address the diverse needs of specific student groups, such as noncredit female Hispanics or reverse-transfer nontraditional single parents. Specific units of a college, such as faculty, single departments, or programs, also could be the focus of research.

When a large number of LSSMs are produced, comparisons can be made across these models. This will provide researchers with the opportunity to generalize knowledge of student success across groups of campuses. In order for such studies to be feasible, mechanisms need to be developed for sharing LSSMs and original data across the academic landscape, among two-year and four-year colleges and high schools as well.

Research is needed to find new approaches for training student services professionals (advisors in particular). A pedagogy of student success needs to be invented to serve as the underlying foundation for the implementation models such as the one shown in Figure 5.2. A pedagogy of student success might include components such as (1) a pedagogy of heuristic knowledge consistent with EMSS, (2) a pedagogy of conation focusing on the student's ability "to apply intellectual energy to the task at hand" (Reitan & Wolfson, 2000, p. 445), as well as to transform cognitive processes into performance (Wild, 1928), and (3) a pedagogy of engagement that promotes student advocacy (Padilla, 2003).

An applied, conation-oriented student success pedagogy may provide scholars and practitioners with new concepts for training student services professionals. It also can drive local innovative action by institutions to enhance student success.

References

Adelman, C. (2006). *The toolbox revisited: Paths to degree completion from high school through college.* Washington, DC: U.S. Department of Education, Office of Vocational and Adult Education.

Adelman, C. (2007). Do we really have a college access problem? *Change, 39*(4). Retrieved July 19, 2007, from http://www.carnegiefoundation.org/change/sub .asp?key = 98&subkey = 2385

Bean, J. P., & Metzner, B. S. (1985). A conceptual model of nontraditional undergraduate student attrition. *Review of Educational Research, 55*(4), 485–540.

Benjamin, M. (1994). The quality of student life: Toward a coherent conceptualization. *Social Indicators Research, 31*(3), 205–264.

Bolge, R. D. (1994a). *Identifying and dealing with access barriers at Mercer County Community College.* (ERIC Document Reproduction Service No. ED376876)

Bolge, R. D. (1994b). *Examination of the learning and psycho-social skills needed by and barriers for remedial students at Mercer Community College.* (ERIC Document Reproduction Service No. ED382240)

Commission on the Future of Higher Education. (2006). *A test of leadership. Charting the future of U.S. higher education.* Washington, DC: U.S. Department of Education, Education Publications Center.

Couturier, L. K. (2006). *Convergence: Trends threatening to narrow college opportunity in America.* Washington, DC: Institute for Higher Education Policy.

Dowd, A. C. (2005). *Data don't drive: Building a practitioner-driven culture of inquiry to assess community college performance.* Indianapolis, IN: Lumina Foundation for Education.

Hagedorn, L. S., Moon, H. S., Maxwell, W., & Pickett, M. C. (2002). *Community college model of student life and retention.* Retrieved February 13, 2007, from http://www.usc.edu/dept/education/truccs/Papers/Interplay_QSL_CC-AERA final3.pdf

Hagedorn, L. S., Perrakis, A. I., & Maxwell, W. (2004). *The negative commandments: Ten ways community colleges hinder student success.* Retrieved April 30, 2005, from http://www.usc.edu/dept/education/truccs/Papers/negative_command ment_final3.pdf

Hardy, D. E., & Katsinas, S. G. (2006). Using community college classifications in research: From conceptual model to useful tool. *Community College Journal of Research & Practice, 30*(4), 339–358.

Kazis, R., & Liebowitz, M. (2003). *Opening doors to earning credentials: Curricular and program format innovations that help low-income students succeed in community colleges.* (ERIC Document Reproduction Service No. ED475990)

Komives, S. R., & Woodard, Jr., D. B. (Eds.). (2003). *Student services* (4th ed.). San Francisco: Jossey-Bass.

LeSure-Lester, G. E. (2003). Effects of coping styles on college persistence decisions among Latino students in two-year colleges. *Journal of College Student Retention,* 5(11), 11–22.

Lynch, R., Harnish, D., & Brown, T. G. (1994). *Seamless education: Barriers to transfer in postsecondary education.* (ERIC Document Reproduction Service No. ED391103)

Miles, M. B., & Huberman, A. M. (1994). *Qualitative data analysis: An expanded sourcebook* (2nd ed.). Thousand Oaks, CA: Sage.

Miller, M. T., Pope, M. L., & Steinmann, T. D. (2005). Dealing with the challenges and stressors faced by community college students: The old try. *Community College Journal of Research and Practice, 29*(1), 63–74.

Myhre, J. R. (1998). *Traveling the transfer path: Student experiences at City College of San Francisco.* (ERIC Document Reproduction Service No. ED416946)

Padilla, R. V. (2003). Reconstructing the Hispanic educational pipeline in the twenty-first century. In R. V. Padilla (Ed.), *Strategic initiatives for Hispanics in higher education: Learning to change* (pp. 35–52). Washington, DC: American Association for Higher Education, Hispanic Caucus.

Padilla, R. V., & Pavel, M. (1986). *Successful Hispanic community college students: An exploratory qualitative study.* Tempe: Arizona State University, Hispanic Research Center.

Padilla, R. V., Treviño, J., Gonzalez, K., & Treviño, J. (1997). Developing local models of minority student success in college. *Journal of College Student Development, 38*(2), 125–135.

Patton, M. Q. (1990). *Qualitative evaluation and research methods* (2nd ed.). Thousand Oaks, CA: Sage.

Reitan, R. M., & Wolfson, D. (2000). Conation: A neglected aspect of neuropsychological functioning. *Archives of Clinical Neuropsychology, 15*(5), 443–453.

Rendón, L. I. (1993). *Validating culturally diverse students: Toward a new model of learning and student development.* (ERIC Document Reproduction Service No. ED371672)

Rendón, L. I. (1995). *Facilitating retention and transfer for first generation students in community colleges.* (ERIC Document Reproduction Service No. ED383369)

Richardson, R. C., Jr., & Skinner, E. F. (1990). Adapting to diversity: Organizational influences on student achievement. *Journal of Higher Education, 61*(5), 485–511.

Stahl, V. V., & Pavel, D. M. (1992). *Assessing the Bean and Metzner model with community college student data.* (ERIC Document Reproduction Service No. ED344639)

Tinto, V. (1987). *Leaving college: Rethinking the causes and cures of student attrition.* Chicago: University of Chicago Press.

Tinto, V. (2002). *Student success and the building of involving educational communities*. Retrieved March 4, 2006, from http://soeweb.syr.edu/Faculty/Vtinto/Files/PromotingStudentSuccess.pdf

Tinto, V. (2006). Research and practice of student retention: What's next? *Journal of College Student Retention, 8*(1), 1–19.

Webb, M. (1989). A theoretical model of community college student persistence. *Community College Review, 16*(4), 42–49.

Wild, E. H. (1928). Influences of conation on cognition, II. *British Journal of Psychology, 18*, 332–355.

6

STUDENT SUCCESS IN A HISPANIC SERVING UNIVERSITY

Raymond V. Padilla and George Norton

I ndividual students seeking a university education often face a challenging campus environment (Attinasi, 1989; Kuh & Love, 2000). According to Kuh, Kinzie, Buckley, Bridges, & Hayek (2006), success for minority students is especially threatened by the barriers they encounter to institutional resources that support academic and personal development. This view is supported by the Lumina Foundation (2006), which reported that "The unfortunate reality is that low income students and students of color do not have adequate access to relevant and timely information about . . . succeeding in college" (p. 1). So it seems that some students do not have the knowledge they need to take effective actions to overcome campus barriers to success.

Other research suggests that campus barriers have a differential and negative impact on the success rates of minority students. Tinto (2003) identified a 22 percent gap between the graduation rate of minority college students and that of majority students. The Lumina Foundation (2006) has further identified "large and expanding . . . negative gaps in college success rates for students of low socioeconomic status and for minority students" (p. 1). Poor minority-student success rates threaten both individual student goals and the realization of state and national goals because the fastest growing population segments (minority and low-income) are the segments that experience the lowest levels of student success (Rendón & Hope, 1996; Texas

Higher Education Coordinating Board, 2000; Western Interstate Commission on Higher Education, 2005). If this trend continues, proportionately fewer minority citizens will have the benefit of a college education, the workforce will be less educated and less prepared for the opportunities of a changing economy, and the flagging economy will have a negative impact on the overall standard of living (Texas Higher Education Coordinating Board, 2000). Thus, there is a compelling interest for researchers to examine more closely the role of campus barriers to student success. This is especially so in Hispanic Serving Institutions (HSIs), which serve a rapidly growing segment of the U.S. population.

Site

The University of Texas at San Antonio (UTSA) is a large public university in a major metropolitan area of the southwestern United States that meets the criteria of a Hispanic Serving Institution (HSI) according to the 1998 amendments to the Higher Education Act of 1965 (Amendments, 1998). As already noted, student success is threatened for historically underrepresented populations in higher education—a category that includes Hispanic and low-income students—by barriers to their benefitting from the institutional resources supporting academic and personal development (Kuh et al., 2006). The student profile at UTSA includes 45.2 percent Hispanic and 54.8 percent non-Hispanic students (UTSA, 2005), and not less than 50 percent of the Hispanic students are considered low income. Therefore, UTSA meets the HSI criteria and is a site that provides a student population suitable for modeling student success at a Hispanic Serving Institution.

A broad sample of participants was selected with the aim of developing an accurate representation of the expertise that successful students use to overcome campus barriers to success. The goal for participant selection was to reflect the broad categories of ethnicity present at UTSA (Patton, 1990) and to "cover as completely as possible the range of experiences likely to exist for the focal group in the target population" (Padilla, 1999, p. 140).

On-campus participant recruitment through the use of fliers, email messages, and direct personal inquiry led to the identification of the sample. Prospective participants who responded to recruitment by making telephone contact with a research team member were screened to eliminate graduate students and freshman undergraduates. Graduate students were screened out because the study examines undergraduate student success. Freshman undergraduate students were excluded because they have a narrower range of experiences when compared to upperclassmen. Prospective participants who were retained in the participant pool were asked by the screener to self-identify as to their race/ethnicity and were directed to either a Hispanic or a non-Hispanic data collection session.

Data Collection and Management

Following the Expertise Model of Student Success, the chief data collection instrument was the unfolding matrix (see chapter 2). This instrument was used to focus the group discussions so that relevant data could be acquired efficiently. Responses by the participants were recorded in the cells of the unfolding matrix to identify the barriers, knowledge, and actions that were attributed to successful students. In addition, student recommendations for changes that UTSA could make to reduce or eliminate barriers also were recorded in the matrix. However, these data are not included in the findings reported here.

Data collection sessions for Hispanic and non-Hispanic participants were arranged in two series of three tandem one-hour sessions. Three focus group sessions enabled Hispanic students to complete an unfolding matrix. Data collection was similar for non-Hispanic students. The Hispanic and non-Hispanic data were collected on separate days. This arrangement of data collection sessions enabled the use of a core local student success model common to both groups but with separate parameter identification for Hispanic and non-Hispanic students.

Students arriving at the data collection sessions were asked to sign the informed consent document required by UTSA's Institutional Review Board. Participants were asked to complete a brief anonymous demographic survey to document the profile of session participants in terms of race/ethnicity, class standing, gender, age, residency status, college trajectory, and major. These steps ensured adherence to UTSA's informed consent regulations and documented the profile of the sample selected for the investigation.

Data management included archiving and providing data security, maintaining the anonymity of the research subjects, and cleaning the data in preparation for data analysis. The collected data were acquired and archived as four distinct data sources for analysis. First, the unfolding matrix captured data in a physical, paper medium. Second, the group interviews were audio recorded to provide redundant and detailed data to support the matrix data. Third, administrative paper records of the research project documented activities of the researchers. Fourth, the data from the unfolding matrix were transcribed into SuperHyperQual© software. This software package was useful for both data management and data analysis.

Security of the data and anonymity of the participants were ensured by storage of paper records, audio recordings, and electronic files under lock and key. Further, electronic files were accessed using password-protected computer programs. Anonymity of the participants was further ensured through the exclusion of participant-identifying information in the research report, and by not using participant names during focus group discussions.

Data cleaning ensured that the data were an accurate representation of what the participants offered in the focus group discussions and involved checking the computerized data set against its original sources. Errors, found by comparing exemplars recorded in the computer program to the corresponding entries on the unfolding matrix, were corrected. Any uncertainties about entries in the unfolding matrix were resolved by examining the audio recordings of the focus group sessions to ensure accuracy. Other data-cleaning steps included verifying that all exemplars were included in the data set and that the spelling of words in the data set was correct. Once the data set was cleaned, data analysis began.

Following EMSS, data analysis consisted of data reduction through the development of taxonomies, and data elaboration through concept modeling (see chapter 2 and Padilla, 1991). Data reduction began with the development of a taxonomy for each column of the unfolding matrix. This noncontingent analysis taxonomizes each matrix column without regard to the taxonomy of barriers. A second data reduction procedure, not used for this study, creates taxonomies by column contingent upon the taxonomy of barriers previously established. Data reduction leads to inductively drawn categories of meaning that can help to develop the local student success model as a concept model. Data elaboration is the production of the actual concept model. In this study, the LSSM concept model is common to both Hispanic and non-Hispanic students, with model parameters specified for each group. Using a common LSSM concept model facilitates the comparison across Hispanic and non-Hispanic groups.

Taxonomic LSSM for Hispanic and Non-Hispanic Students

As already noted, data reduction in EMSS is accomplished by developing taxonomies for three parameters, namely the barriers to student success, the successful students' knowledge base, and the action repertoire of successful students. In this study, taxonomies are reported only for the barriers for Hispanic and non-Hispanic students. However, the raw data for heuristic knowledge and actions for each group are provided as an example of EMSS parameter data before data reduction occurs. Table 6.1 shows the taxonomy of barriers for Hispanic undergraduate students. Table 6.2 shows similar information for non-Hispanic students. For Hispanic students there are six categories of barriers, while there are five categories of barriers for non-Hispanic students. It is instructive that for Hispanic students some of the barriers are connected to the relative newness of the institution and its rapid growth in recent years. Other barriers relate to instructional issues, while still others result from logistical problems and the fact that many Hispanic students are first-generation college students. For non-Hispanic students, academic barriers prevail along with communication issues.

The complete set of exemplars for heuristic knowledge and actions reported by Hispanic and non-Hispanic students are shown in Tables 6.3 and 6.4, respectively. In each table, the first column lists the barriers. The second column details the knowledge that successful students possess to overcome each barrier, while the last column shows the actions that successful students take to overcome each barrier.

LSSM Concept Model

For this study, the general model of student success (GMSS) (see chapter 2) was chosen as the LSSM concept model for both Hispanic and non-Hispanic students (see Figure 6.1). While the core concepts of the model apply to both groups, the model parameters must be identified separately for each group. The model shows that all students arrive on campus with distinct sets of experiences from prior schooling and life in general. These experiences constitute the knowledge base and action repertoire of students as they arrive on campus. While on campus, students experience barriers that must be overcome. If a student's prior experiences resulted in relevant knowledge and actions, then the student can overcome the barriers. Otherwise the student

TABLE 6.1
Taxonomy of Barriers for Hispanic Undergraduates

Barrier Category	Barriers
1. Institutional (im)maturity	1.0 Classes not available 1.1 Wanting to be at UTSA (not just transit through it) 1.2 Outdated technology 1.3 The stigma of UTSA (lack of community) 1.4 Availability of facilities 1.5 Availability of professors 1.6 Large classes
2. Barriers related to faculty	2.0 Language 2.1 Advisor 2.2 Availability of professors 2.3 Professors lack technological skills 2.4 Classes move too fast
3. Barriers related to students	3.0 Language 3.1 Lack of focus 3.2 Choosing a major 3.3 Jobs/jobs related to career 3.4 Transition from high school to college 3.5 Time management 3.6 First generation student 3.7 Financial 3.8 Unsuccessful students 3.9 Transportation 3.10 Classes move too fast
4. Barriers related to academic support (student support services)	4.0 Language 4.1 Lack of focus 4.2 Choosing a major 4.3 First generation student 4.4 Advisor
5. Barriers related to student life	5.0 Transition from high school to college 5.1 First generation student
6. Barriers generally related to student	6.0 Lack of focus 6.1 Jobs/jobs related to career 6.2 Transition from high school to college 6.3 Time management 6.4 First generation student 6.5 Financial 6.6 Transportation

TABLE 6.2
Taxonomy of Barriers for Non-Hispanic Undergraduates

Barrier Category	Barriers
1. Academic	1.0 Communication 1.1 Unrealistic student expectations about degree programs 1.2 Lack of information about degree programs 1.3 Class scheduling 1.4 Lack of information about 2 + 2 programs 1.5 Faculty spread too thin 1.6 Availability of internet classes 1.7 Access to facilities 1.8 Lack of tutoring/T.A. for upper division classes 1.9 Closing classes that are needed 1.10 Access to faculty/advisors 1.11 Classes too large 1.12 Availability of classes 1.13 Advising
2. Personal	2.0 Unrealistic student expectations about degree programs 2.1 Class scheduling 2.2 Jobs 2.3 Partying/Drugs
3. Information	3.0 Communication 3.1 Unrealistic student expectations about degree programs 3.2 Lack of information about degree programs 3.3 Lack of information about 2 + 2 programs 3.4 Communication between students and administration 3.5 Access to faculty/advisors
4. Financial	4.0 Cost 4.1 Jobs
5. Campus	5.0 Parking 5.1 Access to facilities 5.2 Traffic in and around campus 5.3 Uncomfortable temperature in classes

TABLE 6.3
Complete Data Matrix for Hispanic Undergraduate Students

Barriers	Heuristic Knowledge	Actions
1. Language	• Try hard enough • Know peers who have overcome • Shouldn't be afraid to practice • Know resources that can help	• Take intensive E.S.L. classes • Get together with native speakers
2. Lack of focus	• Make priorities • Focus on one thing • Long-range plan • Avoid distractions • Know that they must redirect themselves after temptations • Know that they must strategize • Know that small changes accumulate into large changes • Inspirational materials	• Make a list of things that distract-eliminate • Make study groups • Surround themselves with focused students • Allocate time • Get more sleep • Eat properly • Exercise
3. Choosing a major	• Know to choose a major in which they have skills • Don't just think about salary • Are in touch with current events in a changing world	• Choose a major • Explore different fields in high school • Job shadow • Research • Self-reflection • Graduate undeclared
4. Jobs/jobs related to career	• Know how to prioritize between job and school • Know that they must sacrifice job for school for long-term gain • There is financial aid available • Prioritize living expenses/live on as little as possible • Avoid getting into debt except for financial aid	• Internships • Pick job with quality environment • Network • Know about market demands
5. Transition from high school to college	• Know of students who have successfully made the transition • Having friends with the same transition • Know to plan early for your college career • Not taking too many courses until adjusted • Take core courses early	• Take higher level college credit courses • Learning communities • Start in community college to transition • Go above and beyond in high school
6. Time management	• Know time management techniques • Know to prioritize • Know to space classes • Know to spend time on campus	• Prioritize • Get organized • Divide the work with friends • Make a time schedule • Wake up earlier

(continued)

TABLE 6.3 (Continued)

Barriers	Heuristic Knowledge	Actions
7. First generation student	• Know that they don't want to live paycheck to paycheck • Know the limitations of parents/culture • Know education opens doors to opportunity	• Talk to professors—get a mentor • Go to counselors • Freshman orientation • Think long-term • Get involved • Push away negative attitudes toward college • Join athletics • Become involved in college
8. Financial	• Opportunities to get aid/scholarships • Know how to manage money • Know they have to work to earn money	• Seek help outside of campus (banks) • Capitalize on scholarships, fellowships, research, etc. • Take core courses at CC where it is cheaper • Rearrange courses to make room for job • Accelerate course taking to be marketable • Take marketable courses—certification • Buy groceries instead of eating out • Self-funding events • Undergrad research assistant • Get a job • Use resources from organizations they may be in
9. Advising	• They build relationships with advisors • Know advisors don't have final say • Know advisors are not good with class workload • Plan ahead—sketch out plan • Don't procrastinate in seeking their advisor • Proactive—Responsible for their own plan	• Visit advisor often • Use other resources—online • Use professors as advisors • Seek recommendations from other students • Set appointments with advisors • Know what you want to talk about • Visit professionals in your field • Make appointments in advance • Think about life events and anticipate • Get a second opinion if you get bad advice

TABLE 6.3 (Continued)

Barriers	Heuristic Knowledge	Actions
10. Classes not available	• Plan ahead—know what's offered • Know some students will drop • Know to have a backup plan in case of cancellation • Know to petition to reinstate the course	• Wake up early to register • Seek override • Plan ahead • Pay on time • Timely renewal of financial aid • Attend class to get permission to enroll if others drop • Find a substitute course • Audit course • CLEP class • Take a related course • Take online at another school • Take course remotely • Start a minor • Know the drop dates • Take electives to get those out of the way
11. Wanting to be at UTSA (not just transiting through)	• Invest in the university • Make the best of the campus environment • Know UTSA is a young institution • Know promoting status of UTSA adds value to degree	• Become a part of UTSA • Get involved • Shut out negativity • Promote UTSA to friends and family • Get to know people on campus, professors/students • Start club or organization to get sense of pride • Remember why you came here • Talk to people who went to the university (see that education is similar) • Get on a mission to leave something behind • Work hard to be successful
12. Technology that is outdated	• Know that there is better technology and look for it • Know to do work ahead of time • Know aptitude is more important than technology	• Petition dept. chair • Use labs or colleges that have equipment • Buy own technology • Improvise with resources they are given • Research to check out actual technology

(continued)

TABLE 6.3 (Continued)

Barriers	Heuristic Knowledge	Actions
13. The stigma of UTSA (lack of community)	• Socializing is one-on-one • Know UTSA is trying to build community • Students know that they can develop new organizations/take action to develop community • Get involved in what's available	• Join organizations—fraternity/ sorority • Bypass stigma—remind yourself why you are here • Go to sporting events • Get involved with community building process and learn history of UTSA • Involve family in UTSA • Build relationships with instructors • Live on campus • Involved in larger community and communicate UTSA • Become involved in professional societies • Build cross-organization linkages
14. Unsuccessful students	• Know they won't be around for upper-level courses • Sit up front • Library (with lab) is open 24 hours a day	• Sit up front • Motivate others • Ask questions in class • Meet other people in class • Involve others in discussion • Participate in class • Organize study groups
15. Availability of facilities	• E-mail tutors • Know that there is wireless service • Know availability and work around it	• Find outside resources • Alternatives • Work with administration • Capitalize on campus policies • Be early
16. Availability of professors	• Office hours • Cell phone • Talk after class • Syllabus has contact information • Seek other professors • Know their habits • Ask classmates	• Find another mentor • Work with T/A • Find another professor teaching same class • See them during office hours • Invite them to your organizations • Seek help from peers in class • Go to dept. chair • E-mail • "Stalk" professor (actively seek them)

TABLE 6.3 (Continued)

Barriers	Heuristic Knowledge	Actions
17. Large classes	• Start up study groups/network • Know how to use WebCT • Summer school • Participate in class/ psychologically "shrink it" • Go to S.I. • How to sort through misinformation	• Sit up front • Participate in SI • Exchange number with students around you • Move around classroom to get optimal seat • Ask questions so you'll get noticed • Sit next to active students
18. Professors lack technological skills	• Teach the professors • Know to recommend tech support • Know how to communicate in traditional ways	• Offer to help tutor professor • Work with what they have • Let them know advantages of technology • Offer to be assistant • Give them technology Christmas present • Find another professor
19. Transportation	Data N/A	Data N/A
20. Classes move too fast	Data N/A	Data N/A

will have to develop in real time the knowledge and actions needed to overcome campus barriers. Failure to do so will put the student at risk of dropping out.

Notice that the knowledge component of the LSSM concept model includes both heuristic and academic knowledge. While the unfolding matrix concentrates on heuristic knowledge, it should be clear that each student also must acquire a specific amount of academic knowledge if he or she is to graduate. Usually, the extent and nature of that academic knowledge is spelled out in college catalogs and other official documents. Such academic knowledge has been increasingly well defined over the decades, so today students are required to successfully complete a specific number of credit hours across a variety of courses before they are eligible to graduate.

Finally, it should be noted that the LSSM is a data-driven approach to student success modeling. The model can be focused on the campus as a whole or on any desired subpopulation. The important thing is that the data must be current so that the barriers, knowledge, and actions apply to the students actually enrolled. Too often, student services are provided to meet

TABLE 6.4

Complete Data Matrix for Non-Hispanic Undergraduate Students

Barriers	Heuristic Knowledge	Actions
1. Communication	• Know to be persistent • Know to ask other people • Know to follow up • Know to talk to fellow student	• Get involved on campus • Stay connected • WebCT • Learning instructors' office hours • Attending class
2. Parking	• Know to come early • Know the flow of traffic • Know class schedules • Know where to park • Know there is always a spot in lot 13 • Know parking rules	• Carpooling • Ride shuttle • Take bus • Schedule early classes • Get to campus early
3. Unrealistic student expectations about degree program	• Know what their professors expect of them • Know to proactively seek out information • Know there will be time commitments • Know how they learn/think/study • Ability to comprehend	• Talk to counselor on regular basis • Make a list of questions to ask counselor • Go to career services • Keep records • Have backup plans on classes you want to take
4. Lack of information about degree programs	• Know to talk to faculty • Know to network • Know about resources • Know which catalog you're in • Know your degree plan • Know to schedule your semesters in advance • Know how to read the catalog	• Go to your advisor • Talk to professors that have same degree • Talk to older students • Know information in catalog • Know/Get recommendations about professors to take
5. Class scheduling	• Know your own biological time clock • Know you can discuss your schedule with the department head • Know schedule in advance • Know to be realistic in planning their schedule	• Register early • Plan ahead • Review schedule with advisor • Have backup plan for schedule • Know which professors to take • Know the professors • Spread out difficult classes • Take classes in summer/midterm • CLEP classes

TABLE 6.4 (Continued)

Barriers	Heuristic Knowledge	Actions
6. Cost	• Know about financial resources • Manage their money • Know your financial aid advisor • Know how much it costs (prepare) • Can go to community college for basics	• Fill out scholarships • Apply for financial aid early • Know financial aid counselor • Do an internship • Buy book online • Ask professor if okay to use old edition • Choose a different professor if one requires too many books • Trade books with friends • CLEP
7. Lack of info. about 2 + 2 program	Data N/A	Data N/A
8. Faculty spread too thin	• Prioritize your classes • Downtown classes are available • Go to different sections of same class	• E-mail, find alternative ways to get to know professors • Find alternative ways to become known to professor • Work with T/A
9. Availability of internet classes	• Take Internet courses early on (basics)	• Take Internet courses at community college • Take Internet courses at other universities (make sure it will transfer—confirm it in writing) • Find professors that heavily rely on WebCT • CLEP • Use transfer guide
10. Access to facilities	• Times of operation • Get there early (computer lab) • Know what is offered—available	• Come early • Reserve study spaces early • Learn when facilities are accessible • Find alternatives • Have a backup plan • Don't wait until the last minute
11. Traffic in and around campus	• Park at Valero (lot 13), lot 11 • Arrive before 11 a.m. • Know speed limit on campus • Know construction • Block schedule (plan schedule around parking) • Shuttle schedule • Use shuttle • Shuttle schedule is inconsistent	• Leave early from home, work, etc. • Avoid rush hour • Wait to avoid campus rush times • Build travel time into schedule • Ride shuttle • Prepare for shuttle delays

(continued)

TABLE 6.4 (Continued)

Barriers	Heuristic Knowledge	Actions
12. Lack of information about campus resources	• Don't take everyone's word (students and staff don't always know) • Get involved in campus activities • Network • Build relationships • Take advantage of university workshops	• Get involved • Go online • Get to know website • Explore campus • Use information desk in U.C. • Talk to advisors/professors/other students • Join listserv • Check UTSA e-mail or forward
13. Jobs	• Know your schedule for school and work • Be realistic about time • Priority 1—education, priority 2—job • Jobs are offered on campus • Financial aid can supplement your income	• Plan your schedule—study schedule, class schedule • Find a flexible job • Try to find a job on campus—less travel, more flexible, better hours • Don't overload
14. Lack of tutoring/T.A. for upper division classes	• Your professor can help • Network within your college • Get to know people in your class • Network with professors in your college	• Use professors' office time • Form study groups • Ask professor about extra help, strategies to do well • Talk to other students about how to be successful • Talk to professor about arranging for S.I. or T.A. • Find successful students • Check ratemyprofessor.com—pick carefully
15. Uncomfortable temperature in classes	• Layer • Bring a jacket/parka	• Bring hot beverage
16. Closing classes that are needed	• Talk to department head • Talk to professor teaching class • Take important classes early (don't wait until last semester to take questionable classes) • Get a degree audit • Organize within college to coordinate registration	• Register early • Have back-up plan • Network with other students • Check ASAP to see if people have dropped • Talk to professor • Take class somewhere else

TABLE 6.4 (Continued)

Barriers	Heuristic Knowledge	Actions
17. Communication between students and administration	• Student government • Go to department head • E-mail professor • What the communication avenues are • You can make an appointment with administration • Where are administration offices	• Get to know administration • Look online to see what offices do what • Find faculty phone number online • Go to student ombudsperson
18. Access to faculty/advisors	• Make an appointment • E-mail • They are understaffed • Realistic expectations of F/A • Don't wait until last minute	• Know when they are available • Schedule an appointment • Use their preferred method to contact F/A • Be persistent
19. Class size (too large)	• Honors classes are smaller • Sit up front • Be proactive in contacting the professor • Enroll early	• Come early • Sit up front • Get to know professors • Form study groups
20. Availability of classes	• Know when classes are available • What semester classes are offered • What time classes are offered historically	• Internships • Independent study • Seek course substitution • Take class elsewhere • Stay connected with your advisor • Check with professor about availability
21. Advising	• You can make an appointment with advisor • Make appointment early in the semester • Get a degree audit • E-mail your advisor • You can switch advisors • If in honors college, they provide double coverage	• Get same advisor on consistent basis • Keep a record of what you have done • Be prepared • Visit advisor on a regular basis
22. Partying/drugs	• Know your priorities • Know consequences/policies • How it will affect your grades • There is counseling available on campus	• Say no • Know limits • Moderation • Plan party time • Know who to hang out with • Be responsible • Don't let partying interfere with school work

FIGURE 6.1

The EMSS general student success model parameterized for Hispanic and non-Hispanic students at the subject university. Use of the GMSS as the LSSM concept model provides a common model that facilitates comparisons across the two groups.

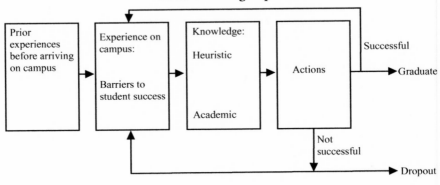

Parameter Table

Parameter	Groups	
	Hispanic	Non-Hispanic
Barriers	Table 6.1	Table 6.2
Heuristic knowledge	Table 6.3	Table 6.4
Academic knowledge	Not parameterized	
Actions	Table 6.3	Table 6.4

the needs of students who may have been on campus in years past, and not the students currently on campus. Keeping the LSSM up to date with current data is one way to overcome this problem.

Implications of the Study

The importance of developing local student success models is that policy, practice, and institutional initiatives intended to improve student success will be driven by data that are current, provided by students and other stakeholders, and from a specific local institution. While extant models of student departure and broad student success theories have both enhanced our under-standing of why students depart college prematurely and identified general conditions in the college environment that are associated with student suc-cess, they have not explained sufficiently what happens inside the "black box" (see chapter 2) of the campus environment that accounts for the gradu-ation of some students while other similar students depart prematurely. Using LSSMs, researchers are able to gain understanding of the unique geog-raphy of barriers that each institution presents to its students, the differential ways that those barriers impact particular segments of the student population (or even the entire student population), and how successful students over-come barriers to their success. Faculty and staff, using local data, can make improvements in policy and practice that reduce or eliminate student success barriers, including those faced by targeted student subpopulations. These initiatives and improvements have the potential to be effective because they are based on data pertinent to the actual students on the local campus rather than on generalized data collected at other campuses. In other words, the LSSM approach offers a specific model that explains the phenomenon of student success at a particular campus. In addition, such a model can be used as a tool for improving student success.

These remarks about local student success modeling resonate with the observations of some student success researchers regarding the state of cur-rent research in the field. For example, Tinto and Pusser (2006) join Hearn (2006) in arguing that the recommendations from current research may not be pertinent to individual institutions, because they are generalized from re-search that is based on other institutions. Hearn (2006) and Rendón (2006) recommend that empirical data inform models of student success, and sug-gest a qualitative methodology for development of theory to explain the phe-nomenon of student success. By extension, institutional efforts intended to improve student success should be informed by timely local student data that can point campus leaders to the policy challenges that are most salient for student success on their particular campus.

AUTOETHNOGRAPHIC ENCOUNTER:
A PERSONAL STAKE (BY GEORGE NORTON)

Modeling student success at a particular institution is more than a research interest for me. It intersects my life in multiple ways. My work at the time of this writing is in admissions and orientation at the University of Texas at San Antonio, a large public university in the Southwest that struggles with low rates of student success. This situation provides ample incentive for me to find out what happens inside the black box (described in chapter 2) that results in some students departing through the graduation channel while too many others depart campus through the dropout channel. Moreover, I am someone who, by some measures, would be considered a dropout. Having completed doctoral coursework at a major research institution on the East Coast, I arrived at UTSA not having persisted to graduation from the doctoral program. I am fortunate to have been provided an opportunity to resume my doctoral studies in a new location, to find the need for this line of inquiry, and to find faculty who have developed the conceptual framework and research methods to guide my research. I also have found faculty who share my interests and want to partner with me while guiding me toward reaching my educational goals.

This personal, professional, and research interest in modeling student success at a university created a challenge for me, namely the need to keep separate my various roles—researcher, student, and administrator—during the data collection process. After all, although the participants and I study at different levels, I too am a student at the same institution, and I am interested in achieving my educational goals just as they are. Chapter 2 emphasizes the role of the focus group moderator during data collection, indicating that "The moderator should help the individual to articulate what he or she is trying to say without substituting the moderator's own words or ideas for those of the interviewee" (p. 32). I would add, based on the experience of being a moderator, that it is important to refrain from playing the role of consensus builder when focus group members respond to each other and "self-correct" their statements based on the statements of others. The goal for data collection is not to collect exemplars of group consensus; rather, it is to collect exemplars of individual student perspectives about barriers to student success, of the knowledge successful students possess that helps them to overcome barriers, and of the actions they take to overcome barriers. I think that having a deep, even personal, interest in a research topic is a benefit. But I also think that it is critical to maintain an appropriate researcher perspective in order to enhance the validity of the results and to increase their viability, for the purpose of accurately informing institutional initiatives to improve student success.

References

Amendments to the Higher Education Act of 1965, Pub. L. No. 105–244. (1998).

Attinasi, L. C. (1989). Getting in: Mexican Americans' perceptions of university attendance and the implications for freshman year persistence. *The Journal of Higher Education, 60*(3), 247–277.

Hearn, J. C. (2006, November). *Student success: What research suggests for policy and practice.* Paper presented at the National Symposium on Postsecondary Student Success: Spearheading a Dialog on Student Success, Washington, DC.

Kuh, G. D., Kinzie, J., Buckley, J. A., Bridges, B. K., & Hayek, J. C. (2006, November). *What matters to student success: A review of the literature.* Paper presented at the National Symposium on Postsecondary Student Success: Spearheading a Dialog on Student Success, Washington, DC.

Kuh, G. D., & Love, P. G. (2000). A cultural perspective on student departure. In J. M. Braxton (Ed.), *Reworking the student departure puzzle* (pp. 196–212). Nashville, TN: Vanderbilt University Press.

Lumina Foundation for Education. (2006). *What we know about access and success in postsecondary education: Informing Lumina Foundation's strategic direction.* Retrieved February 22, 2006, from http://www.luminafoundation.org/research/what_we_knowendnotes/wwk_fuldoc.html

Padilla, R. V. (1991). Assessing heuristic knowledge to enhance college students' success. In G. D. Keller, J. R. Deneen, & R. J. Magallan (Eds.), *Assessment and access* (pp. 81–92). Albany: State University of New York Press.

Padilla, R. V. (1999). College student retention: Focus on success. *Journal of College Student Retention, 1*(2), 131–145.

Patton, M. Q. (1990). *Qualitative evaluation and research methods* (2nd ed.). Thousand Oaks, CA: Sage.

Rendón, L. I., & Hope, R. O. (1996). An educational system in crisis. In L. I. Rendón & R. O. Hope (Eds.), *Educating a new majority: Transforming America's educational system for diversity* (pp. 1–32). San Francisco: Jossey-Bass.

Rendón, L. I. (2006, November). *Reconceptualizing success for underserved students in higher education.* Paper presented at the National Symposium on Postsecondary Student Success: Spearheading a Dialog on Student Success, Washington, DC.

Texas Higher Education Coordinating Board. (2000). *Closing the gaps: The Texas higher education plan.* Retrieved November 4, 2005, from http://www.thecb.state.tx.us/reports/PDF/0379.PDF

Tinto, V. (2003). Establishing conditions for student success. In L. Thomas, M. Cooper, & J. Quinn (Eds.), *Improving completion rates among disadvantaged students* (pp. 1–10). Sterling, VA: Trentham Books Limited.

Tinto, V., & Pusser, B. (2006, November). *Moving from theory to action: Building a model of institutional action for student success.* Paper presented at the National

Symposium on Postsecondary Student Success: Spearheading a Dialog on Student Success, Washington, DC.

University of Texas at San Antonio. (2005). *Fall semester 2005 student profile*. Retrieved February 16, 2006, from http://www.utsa.edu/Registrar/stats/2005/fall/page06.html

Western Interstate Commission on Higher Education (WICHE). (2005). *Knocking on the college door*. Boulder, CO: Author.

7

IMPLEMENTATION MODELS

Taking systematic action within the life world entails the recognition, development, and use of conjugate models as shown in Figure 1.3 (chapter 1). With reference to Figure 1.3, the expertise model of student success can be seen as the theoretical model that occupies the upper left-hand quadrant of the figure. The local student success model, including the taxonomic LSSM and its associated concept model, can be seen as the empirical model that is shown in the lower left-hand quadrant of Figure 1.3. The theoretical (general) model provides an explanation of the problem at hand and specifies the relevant parameters, which can vary across different instances of the theoretical model as it is applied at specific locations. Whereas the theoretical model specifies the parameters as constructs, the empirical model provides actual values for the model parameters based on local observations. Hence, every empirical model is local in the sense that the general parameters of the theoretical model are given specific values that are determined within the boundaries of some observable space and within a specific period of time. More formally, the empirical model is an instantiation of the theoretical model within a bounded segment of the life world.

Yet, the empirical model by itself does not automatically lead to action in the life world. The empirical model does provide insight into how the problem at hand can be understood locally given the theoretical framework that has been selected. In short, the empirical model can be used to inform systematic action, but it does not constitute action in itself. In Figure 1.3 systematic action resides in the lower right-hand quadrant and requires an implementation model that is linked to the models in the other three quadrants along with the larger metainfluences that also are in play. Implementation models are results oriented and depend heavily on a feasible action plan and the availability of adequate resources (along with a supportive policy environment). For this reason, evaluation of the results of the implementation model is always a concomitant aspect of systematic action. This chapter describes one example of an implementation model based on EMSS and the LSSM that was developed at a large public university in the Southwest.

Implementation Model Example

The Local Situation

Located in a large urban area of the Southwest, this public university had experienced very rapid growth in student enrollment. Unfortunately, graduation rates among undergraduate students were low, with many students taking five, six, or more years to graduate. The university came under pressure from its governing board to improve graduation rates both in terms of the percentage of students graduating and the number of years that it took for them to graduate. Not surprisingly, the political pressure exerted by the governing board found its way into the student affairs administration of the university, where the need arose to contemplate changing significantly the way student services were provided.

Since the problem of low graduation rates was particularly acute for racial and ethnic minority students, student affairs administrators wanted to focus attention on these groups. Over the years, the university had established quite a number of programs to deal with the special problems encountered by racial and ethnic minority students. Most of these programs had been created in response to specific constituencies that had demanded greater access and opportunity from the university. Thus, the constellation of programs dedicated to these groups reflected little regard for efficient use of resources and careful monitoring of results. On the other hand, each program had developed its own group of advocates both within and outside of the university, so that making any changes to these programs was likely to be seen by one group or another as a threat and a cause for political mobilization. Such was the situation for key student affairs administrators when they turned to the author for help in improving student services programs, including those that served racial and ethnic minority students. The number of identifiable student services programs was about 15, with 3 or 4 dedicated specifically to minority students. The challenge was to use EMSS to bring about improvement in services for students, including minority students, at this large urban university, with the general goal of increasing graduation rates.

Collecting Data

The first order of business was to collect data within the framework of EMSS. Undergraduate students completed four unfolding matrices. A sample of students from all student services programs completed the first matrix in order to get a general picture of how students were experiencing the campus. Table 7.1 shows the characteristics of the students who participated in the three dialogue groups for this matrix. Ethnicity was self-identified. Most of the students under the "other" category appeared to be international students. Students were volunteers and included a mix of majority, ethnic/racial minority, and special needs students (reentry adults, disabled, etc.).

The second matrix was completed by students who participated in a minority assistance program that served various ethnic and racial minorities, including African Americans, Hispanics, and Asian Americans. The characteristics of the student sample for this matrix are shown in Table 7.2.

The third matrix included only students who participated in a program for Native American students. Table 7.3 shows the characteristics of this sample.

TABLE 7.1
Characteristics of Students for Sample from All Student Services Programs

	Group 1 (n = 9)	*Group 2 (n = 8)*	*Group 3 (n = 8)*
Male	5	4	3
Female	4	4	5
Sophomore	2	1	0
Junior	3	1	1
Senior	4	6	7
African American	1	2	1
Asian American	0	0	1
Latino	4	1	1
Native American	0	0	0
White	2	3	4
Other	2	2	1

TABLE 7.2

Characteristics of Students for Sample from the Minority Assistance Program

	All Groups (n = 24)
Male	7
Female	17
Freshman	2
Sophomore	7
Junior	7
Senior	8
African American	4
Asian American	2
Latino	18
Native American	0
White	0

TABLE 7.3

Characteristics of Students for Sample from the Native American Program

	All Groups (n = 12)
Male	2
Female	10
Freshman	4
Sophomore	2
Junior	5
Senior	1

The fourth matrix was completed by high school students, all females, who were participating in a special program for mothers and daughters. All of the participants were Hispanic (mostly Mexican American) and numbered 14 across all groups.

The LSSM concept model for the first matrix (all student services programs) is shown in Figure 2.8 (chapter 2). The taxonomy of barriers includes four categories: personal characteristics, transition, communication, and instruction. These categories of barriers are used to develop a concept model that shows how the students experience the campus. In brief, students arrive on campus and face barriers incident to each student's personal background characteristics related to language, family, community, culture, etc. At the same time, the students experience a transition from high school to college, which has its own set of barriers. In dealing with all of these barriers, the students' communication skills come into play. However, communication itself can be a barrier, so students must deal with communication barriers even as they attempt to use communication skills to overcome other barriers. How the student is able to deal with all of these barriers then influences how the student manages barriers related to instruction. One can see clearly from this model that barriers in the academic arena are encountered by the student in the context of myriad other barriers that are not academic. This is a dynamic model, so time flows from left to right. Moreover, the model also shows (at the bottom) that the student experience on campus is mediated for better or worse by the knowledge, services, and resources provided by a number of players, including family, friends, community, and various student services programs on campus.

An Implementation LSSM

As has been noted already, neither EMSS (the general model) nor the LSSM leads directly to action by the institution. One reason is that EMSS is a theoretical model that captures one understanding of what happens when students experience a campus. The LSSM simply takes that understanding and shows what is happening on some specific campus. From an institution's point of view, these models both apply to the cognitive, rather than to the conative (action), domain. Another reason these models don't lead directly to action is that EMSS focuses largely on the student, what the student experiences, what the student knows, and what the student does; what still is needed is a model for action—not for the student, but for the institution. Such a model would take notice of the LSSM and be responsive to it, but the focus of the implementation model clearly has to be the institution.

This means that it is necessary to understand what the institution is doing with respect to the student experience on campus. Formally, the mission of the institution is to accept, instruct, support, and graduate students.

Support generally involves offering to students a variety of student services on campus that, in terms of EMSS, are designed to help the students overcome recognized barriers to their success. Taken as a whole, such services typically involve three main activities: providing information to students (e.g., orientation, career counseling, etc.), providing an actual service or at least making a referral (e.g., financial aid, health services, etc.), and monitoring student actions and results. Based on this understanding of student services, an implementation model like the one shown in Figure 7.1 can be developed. Notice that this model integrates elements from EMSS and in particular from the LSSM developed for the subject campus.

The implementation model assumes two foci: the student and the institutionally provided services. The student focus is framed within the EMSS perspective: The goal of the student is to use expertise to overcome campus barriers in order to make academic progress and eventually to graduate. The actual barriers vary depending on the campus and the population sample that completed the unfolding matrix (the barriers shown in the figure are for the sample of all student services programs in the subject campus). The student experience is mediated by student services, the second focus shown in the model. As already noted, any given student services program is either informing, serving, or monitoring some group of students. Within the context of EMSS, this service function aims to influence a student's heuristic knowledge or action repertoire so that the student's chances of overcoming barriers are enhanced. In the case in which an actual service is provided, the barrier may be overcome directly through student services intervention.

FIGURE 7.1
An Implementation LSSM Focusing on Student Services and Student Success

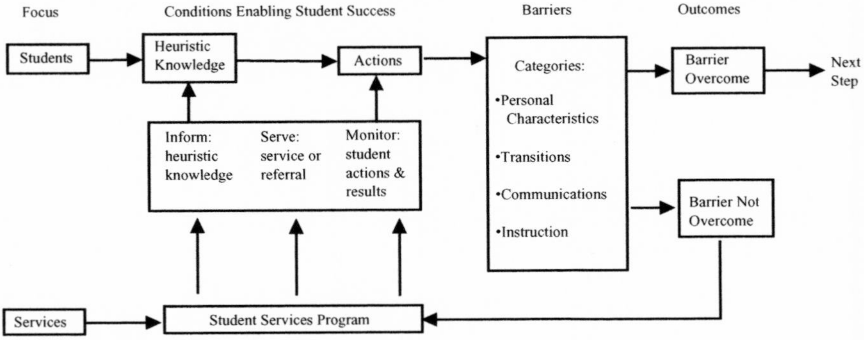

Notice that monitoring of students is a prominent feature of this implementation model. Such monitoring is needed especially when student services consist of enhancing student expertise (knowledge and action). If a student fails to acquire the proper information or to take effective action based on that information, it is unlikely that the student will overcome whatever barriers he or she is facing. So monitoring of the student is essential.

Implicit in the implementation model is the idea that student services must address the barriers that their current students are actually facing. The unfolding matrix provides a tool for identifying the geography of barriers for the campus as a whole or for any given subpopulation. Too often, student services on campus are designed to address barriers for students who once attended the institution but who are no longer the dominant type of student on campus. With changing demographics and historic changes in society, it is often the case that new students with different needs are left underserved. One way to realign student services with actual student needs is to make sure that all student services programs on campus are addressing the barriers identified by their current students. This realignment entails at least two distinct but related strategies: (1) a comprehensive self-assessment of each student service and (2) an action plan to refocus all student services so that the services are responsive to current barriers on campus.

The Self-Assessment

There are two aspects to the self-assessment. First, each student service is canvassed to determine how it addresses the barriers that students identified. This self-assessment can be seen as a mapping of the barriers as related to the activities of each service. Second, each service is given the opportunity to take on any of the barriers as part of its mission. Figure 7.2 shows a prototypical instrument that can be used to conduct the barriers-mapping exercise.

In general, this form includes all the barriers identified through the unfolding matrix for a given campus. In the illustration, the barriers listed are those that were identified by students in the minority assistance program on the subject campus. Therefore, this form would be appropriate for the self-assessment of all services provided through the minority assistance program. Given a relevant list of barriers, the form can be modified for use by any given service or program. Using this form, the administrator of a student service identifies the current priority for each barrier in terms of the actual services being delivered. A five-point Likert scale is used to express priority,

FIGURE 7.2

Prototypical Assessment Form to Map Barriers into Student Services

Program Self-Assessment: MAAP Program Cluster Mapping Barriers to Service Activities and Goals			
Service or Program Name: Contact: Phone: Email: Date: Page ___ of ___			
Barriers	Current Priority	Goal Priority*	Feasibility**
MP1 Financial	1 2 3 4 5	1 2 3 4 5	1 2 3 4 5
MP2 Peer pressure	1 2 3 4 5	1 2 3 4 5	1 2 3 4 5
MP3 Lack of support (family/instructors)	1 2 3 4 5	1 2 3 4 5	1 2 3 4 5
MP4 Prioritizing	1 2 3 4 5	1 2 3 4 5	1 2 3 4 5
MP5 Time	1 2 3 4 5	1 2 3 4 5	1 2 3 4 5
MP6 Racial discrimination	1 2 3 4 5	1 2 3 4 5	1 2 3 4 5
MP7 Lack of self-confidence	1 2 3 4 5	1 2 3 4 5	1 2 3 4 5
MP8 Family issues	1 2 3 4 5	1 2 3 4 5	1 2 3 4 5
MP9 Stress	1 2 3 4 5	1 2 3 4 5	1 2 3 4 5
MP10 Networking (to avoid seclusion)	1 2 3 4 5	1 2 3 4 5	1 2 3 4 5
MP11 Being first-generation college student	1 2 3 4 5	1 2 3 4 5	1 2 3 4 5

*1, 2 = lower priority—No resources allocated
  3, 4, 5 = higher priority—Some resources allocated

**1 = low
   5 = high

with the chief criterion being the level of resources currently being expended to address each barrier. The second column allows the service administrator to indicate the priority that each barrier would receive if the administrator could rearrange priorities. This column is labeled "goal priority." In effect, this exercise allows the service administrator to assess which barriers, if any, actually are being addressed with services, and to indicate how the administrator would rearrange priorities if given the opportunity to do so. The third column seeks the administrator's view as to the feasibility of addressing each barrier through the service under assessment. While priority for addressing a barrier may be high, there still may be reasons why actual service delivery for that barrier would not be feasible through the service program under assessment. Barriers with high priority but low feasibility may indicate the need to significantly restructure service programs or to start new ones capable of addressing the indicated barriers.

After mapping barrier priorities, the second aspect of the self-assessment is to describe each service in the context of the barriers identified on campus. Figure 7.3 shows a prototypical form that may be used for this part of the self-assessment. The form captures a brief description of the service provided. Here a current or proposed service can be entered. For the service described, the administrator indicates the focus of the service. Note that the four categories of service are consistent with the local implementation model already discussed. Next, the administrator identifies the specific barriers that are being addressed by the service. These are the same barriers as those identified by the students when completing an unfolding matrix.

The current priority and goal priority for each barrier are identified. In addition, the administrator provides a specific recommendation for the

FIGURE 7.3
Prototypical Assessment Form to Describe Services and Resource Allocation

Program Self-Assessment
Description of Services and Resource Allocation

Program Name: Page ___ of ___

Description of service activity:

Type of service(s). Check all that apply for service activity described above:

___Heuristic knowledge acquisition by students
___Provide actual service
___Provide referral for service
___Monitor student actions and results

Barrier(s) addressed: Current Priority: Goal Priority:

Number of students who need service: Number of students actually being served:

Strategic action for this service:
___Keep current level of service
___Increase level of service—Number of additional students to be served:
___Decrease level of service—Number of students that will not be served:
___Eliminate (Explain why in Description above.)
___New service (Explain need in Description above.)

Resources (for this service)

	FTE Professional	FTE Staff	FTE Student Help	Operating Costs
Current:				
Proposed:				

service that is being described. This recommendation allows upper-level administrators to consider eliminating the service, maintaining the current level of service, increasing or decreasing the level of service, or starting a new service. Whatever the case, the service provided will be mapped into the barriers being addressed. A crucial step is to link service delivery to the resource allocation process. Therefore, each service must indicate the current and proposed level of resource allocation in terms of staff and operating dollars.

The self-assessment is done at the service-program level, but it can easily roll up all the way to senior administrators who must determine overall service priorities and resource allocation. This exercise, together with the action plan, provides a means to rationally reallocate existing resources or to strategically deploy new ones as student barriers to success are addressed by the institution.

The Action Plan

Given a robust self-assessment, development of the action plan is a straightforward activity. The key is to link continuing and new service programs to current barriers and to allocate resources accordingly. The process is field sensitive in the sense that lower-level staff and administrators have the opportunity to indicate their priorities for addressing barriers as well as the amount of resources that they believe will be necessary to do the job. Given this information, middle- and upper-level administrators can set the institution-wide priorities and distribute resources in a way that responds to their own priorities, available resources, and constraints. Development of the action plan starts with an exercise in which student services administrators propose continuing and new services that are responsive to relevant barriers. Figures 7.4 and 7.5 show prototypical forms that can be used to propose continuing or new service programs. The two forms are very similar, but the idea is to separate continuing student services from proposed new ones.

Each form provides for a description of the service that will be provided by selecting from the types of services indicated in the implementation model. In addition, a service category is assigned to each service. The relevant categories are *common*, *targeted*, and *cross-targeted services*. Common services are services that can apply to virtually any student on campus. Targeted services apply to some targeted group of students (e.g., reentry students, freshmen, etc.). These services are responsive to the special needs of some students. Cross-targeted services can apply to more than one group of special

FIGURE 7.4
Prototypical Form for Proposing a Continuing Service

Student Services Delivery Action Plan
Continuing Services

Year(s):   to

Program Name: Page ___ of ___

Contact: Tele:
Email:

Description of service activity:

Type of service(s). Check all that apply for service activity described above:
___Heuristic knowledge acquisition by students
___Provide actual service
___Provide referral for service
___Monitor student actions and results

Service category:
___Common (all students)
___Targeted (identify target group):
___Cross-targeted (identify target groups):

Barrier(s) addressed (include priority):

Number of students who need service:
Number of students to be served:

Current Resources Allocated (for this service)

FTE Professional	FTE Staff	FTE Student Help	Operating Costs

needs students (e.g., minority students). By carefully identifying the category of service, an institution can make sure that common student needs are met with common services, and special student needs are met with targeted services. The idea is to develop a system of service delivery that is both effective and efficient. Student services are effective when they address both common and special needs. They are efficient when unnecessary duplication of services is avoided. Economies of scale can be achieved when targeted services can be clustered to meet the needs of more than one targeted subpopulation (i.e., cross-targeted services).

FIGURE 7.5
Prototypical Form for Proposing a New Service

Student Services Delivery Action Plan
New Services

Year(s):   to

Program Name: Page ___ of ___
Contact: Tele:
Email:

Description of NEW service activity:

Type of service(s). Check all that apply for service activity described above:
___Heuristic knowledge acquisition by students
___Provide actual service
___Provide referral for service
___Monitor student actions and results

Service category:
___Common (all students)
___Targeted (identify target group):
___Cross-targeted (identify target groups):

Barrier(s) addressed (include priority):

Number of students who need service:
Number of students to be served:

New Resources Proposed (for this service)

FTE Professional	FTE Staff	FTE Student Help	Operating Costs

The careful deployment of services can be an antidote to two problems commonly found in student services: (1) neglect of the needs of identifiable subpopulations, and (2) unnecessary duplication of services in an effort to serve targeted groups. Failure to meet student needs leaves the students unassisted as they struggle to overcome barriers. In the worst case, badly provided services just add more barriers for the students. On the other hand, unnecessary duplication can be seen when institutions attempt to respond to the needs of special populations using the "mushroom model": They simply keep adding new services, increasing administrative overhead, with little attention to the articulation of services and their efficacy.

Each form gives the service provider the opportunity to indicate which barriers are being addressed and their priority. In addition, some sense of the need for the service is provided by indicating the number of students who need the service and the number of students who actually will be served. Budget information is entered at the bottom of the form. This budget information can be aggregated across all services supervised by one administrator so that administrators upstream can make resource allocation decisions. Figure 7.6 provides a prototypical form for summarizing resources across services.

The resources summary form helps the service-delivery-program administrator to develop an operating budget that is responsive to current student barriers on campus given the priorities assigned. This information can be rolled up to middle- and upper-level student affairs administrators, who can

FIGURE 7.6
Prototypical Form for Summarizing Resources Across Services

Student Services Delivery Action Plan
Summary of Resources

Program Name: Year(s)   to

Contact: Tele:
Email:

Service Activity (Continuing)	FTE Professional	FTE Staff	FTE Student Help	Operating Costs
Total (Continuing)				
Service Activity (New)				
Total (New)				
Grand Total				

make budget allocation decisions aimed at maximizing student success. Clearly, through this process, middle- and upper-level administrators have the opportunity to shape the allocation and reallocation of resources to fit overall institutional goals. At the same time, lower-level administrators who are responsible for actually delivering services have the opportunity to develop strategic approaches to service delivery based on current data about student needs.

AUTOETHNOGRAPHIC ENCOUNTER: THE NEED FOR ADMINISTRATIVE PROWESS

It was with some trepidation that I accepted the assignment to assist a large urban university to revamp its student services programs in order to help more students to be successful. I had imagined that, after years of developing what I then called the "student success model," it would be a straightforward matter for student affairs administrators to "just do it." As I was doing the development work, I made sure that certain middle-level administrators received copies of my reports, hoping that they might be inspired to enact improvements. But little was changed as far as I could see. The mushroom model of student services was very much in evidence. It was not until political pressure led to demands for improvement in student graduation rates that finally my administrator friends came calling.

After I accepted the assignment to help improve student success, I quickly realized that the task was not as straightforward as I had imagined it. The key issue for me was that the LSSM was conceptual and did not really provide a roadmap for institutional action. In other words, the LSSM was necessary, but not sufficient, to effect change. What was needed was an implementation LSSM that would include the conceptual LSSM but that would go beyond it in terms of guiding action. That is how the idea of a self-assessment and an action plan came about. Later, when I reflected on how the process had unfolded, I realized that in order to come up with an implementation LSSM I had unconsciously shifted from researcher to administrator. Having spent more than a dozen years in university administration, I had learned how to manage academic programs. It was these program management skills that came in handy as I thought about the implementation LSSM.

After we completed the self-assessment and the action plan, it became clear to me that all we really had was a large volume of hopefully valuable information. What was really needed at this point was effective administrative action based on that information. I realized that I had reached the limits of what I could do as a researcher. At the end of the day, some administrator has to take the bull by the horns and do something. Solid and relevant information is critical to effective action, but because administration is more art than science, an administrator has to take many things into account as actions are contemplated. In short, effective administrative action requires administrative prowess. Such prowess includes information-handling skills as well as the creative impulse to do things in novel ways, which always entails risk. A well-informed administrator is not enough. He or she must be able to think in new ways to determine what is feasible and to assess risk.

I made this point very clearly to my administrator colleagues. I'm sure that this was not an easy time for them. I told them, basically, "The time has come for you to do something." Since their priority was to revamp the services that were being provided to minority students, that became their focus. They finally proposed a reorganization of minority student services based on the idea of a multicultural services center where they could focus on delivering targeted and cross-targeted student services, avoiding unnecessary duplication with common student services provided elsewhere on campus. In other words, it appears that they latched on to the idea of efficacy and efficiency discussed in this chapter. A couple of years later, I checked on their work, and apparently they were fairly pleased with the results.

8

EXPANDING THE
CONVERSATION

The rising interest in student success (Attewell & Lavin, 2007; Colley, 2007; Zeidenberg, Jenkins, & Calcagno, 2007) is evident in events such as the 2006 National Symposium on Student Success that was sponsored by the National Postsecondary Education Cooperative (NPEC) in Washington, D.C. In some ways, this event was an invitation to engage and expand the conversation on student success modeling. The previous chapters in this book are just one example of how the conversation can be expanded. However, there are still a number of topics and issues that merit additional comment with the aim of strengthening research and practice. In this chapter some of those topics and issues will be introduced. They include issues related to the use of qualitative and quantitative data, aspects of comparative studies on student success, the status of dropout studies, and the need to revisit complexity and conjugate models in the contexts of both research and practice and advancing the field. Additional topics include the microstructure of student success, the inclusion of the affective domain in student success models, and a potential new role for the student affairs profession. The hope is that others will enter the conversation and engage these and similar issues from multiple perspectives. Perhaps this will advance the field in new and unexpected ways.

Bridging the Qualitative and Quantitative Divide

It was mentioned in passing in chapter 2 that EMSS to date has been based on qualitative data, in particular the "qualitative survey." There are good reasons for using qualitative methods in EMSS. First, while EMSS includes a general model of student success, it actually emphasizes local models in order to maximize the relevance of the barriers for any given campus. This emphasis on particularity is a hallmark and strength of qualitative research, so it naturally lends itself to EMSS. Second, if barriers to student success are identified *a priori* (as is typically done in quantitative studies), those barriers usually come from somewhere outside of the subject campus. This always raises the question of the relevance of those barriers, given that normally it has not been established that they are the barriers actually present in the subject campus. Qualitative methods avoid this problem entirely. Third, underlying EMSS is expert systems thinking, where the issue of compiling an expert knowledge base is not trivial. In EMSS the students are seen as experts, so it is necessary to extract the expert knowledge base that resides mostly in their heads. Qualitative methods are well suited for the purpose of extracting a knowledge base.

In spite of the clear strengths of qualitative methods, these methods do not address some important concerns, including salience and scale. Salience has to do with the prevalence of barriers on campus. While students can identify a barrier using the unfolding matrix technique, there is little or no information as to how many students on campus might actually experience that barrier. Here is a case in which quantity can make a significant difference, particularly when action strategies are being developed. The extreme case would be when only one or a handful of students experience some identified barrier. What should be the level of institutional response if only a few students are affected? In some cases (for example, in the case of star athletes) it may be important to address a barrier even when only a few students are affected. In other cases, such barriers may be given a lower priority when resources are limited. Another extreme would be when the vast majority of students experience some barrier. In this case, the institution might assign a high priority to eliminating or lessening that barrier. So salience is very important in the action arena, and quantitative methods seem to be best suited for assessing the salience of barriers. The availability of salience data would enrich the taxonomic LSSMs by projecting (assuming a suitable sample) the distribution of each barrier across the relevant student population in the subject campus.

It should be evident that the LSSM concept models produced with qualitative methods are scale free (Barabasi, 2003). This means that relationships between concepts in the models can be stated only in directional terms. The strength of relationships between concepts cannot be expressed very well using qualitative data. On the other hand, scaled models routinely estimate the strength of relationships between concepts. To create scaled models requires the use of quantitative measures for each of the key concepts in the model. So, here again, quantitative data can be used advantageously to develop scaled models of student success. With scaled models it also is possible to assess the models themselves to determine the fit between a model and the phenomenon to which it applies. This can be a valuable tool for the advancement of theory, since all qualitative models are interpretive, and some external means of evaluating them is needed. Moreover, any given data set can lead to rival models of the phenomenon being studied. A tool that can help to assess the fit of competing models would be quite useful for both the advancement of theory and the development of action strategies.

Given the advantages of both qualitative and quantitative data, one strategy to incorporate both strengths in student success modeling would be to use mixed methods research designs. Such designs would start with a study to develop the qualitative LSSMs for a given campus. A second study then would scale the LSSMs to determine the salience of barriers and to examine relationships between concepts as well as the overall fit of the LSSM concept model. This type of research would go hand in hand with the development of implementation models designed to lead to greater student success on a given campus. All that has been said so far would apply both to the student population on campus as a whole and to particular subpopulations, depending on the samples used. By focusing on subpopulations, action strategies can be fine tuned to meet special needs. In addition, the availability of scaled models would permit the detailed comparison of student success models across various subpopulations.

Comparative Studies

Chapter 3 provides an example of a comparative study that uses student success modeling in a qualitative mode. Using EMSS qualitatively, the tools available for comparative studies are the set of barriers, the knowledge base, and the action repertoire that are identified for a given group. When these data are elaborated through data reduction and synthesis, the taxonomic and concept model LSSMs also can be used as tools for making comparisons. In chapter 3, the main tool for comparing the high-performing and the non-high-performing elementary schools is the LSSM concept models. In chapter 6, where the same LSSM concept model is used for the two comparison groups, the main tool for comparison is the set of barriers (and resulting taxonomy) for each group. These and similar comparisons are based on scale-free models of student success.

However, as noted above, it may be feasible to augment scale-free data and models if additional quantitative data are collected to obtain scaled data and models. Using quantitative data, a whole range of other comparison tools becomes available. Quantitative data will permit comparisons between groups and campuses on the relevance and salience of barriers. Such comparisons will shed light on differences between groups in terms of which barriers are relevant to various groups and how salient the barriers are for each group. Information related to relevance and salience is important in the formulation of action strategies to promote student success. Moreover, scaled models can provide additional tools for evaluating the efficacy of action strategies that have been implemented to increase student success. Program success might be assessed, not only in terms of increased student retention and graduation rates (which are typically long-term measures), but specifically in terms of the decrease in the salience of barriers within a population of interest or the actual elimination of specific barriers. Scaled data can provide metrics for these benchmarks, which can be used effectively over shorter time horizons.

With scaled data it also may be possible finally to tease out how the barriers prevalent on one campus play out on a different campus. It will be necessary first to identify the set of barriers present on one campus using the unfolding matrix to gather these qualitative data. Next, the prevalence of those barriers would be assessed by conducting a standard quantitative survey on campus. To make a comparison it would be necessary to conduct the same quantitative survey on a second campus. The resulting scaled data for the two campuses provide the basis for comparison. By collecting suitable demographic and background data in the surveys, more subtle comparisons can be made between the two campuses.

Notice that this quantitative comparison procedure says nothing about possible barriers that are unique to the second campus. Unique barriers would require the collection of qualitative data on the second campus. However, the comparison technique does make it possible to identify a set of barriers that is common to more than one campus. Such general barriers can be used to develop student success models that cover a range of campuses or to implement action strategies related to groups of campuses or entire educational systems. Using similar logic, scaled data and models could be used to identify differences in barriers at various levels of the educational system so that one could develop a more global view of how students experience the educational system from beginning to end.

Dropout Models in New Perspective

While the interest in student success recently has been gaining ground over the interest in student dropout, it is worthwhile to pause to assess the relevance of dropout studies. As shown in Figure 1.2 (chapter 1), dropout and success studies are logically linked. Examining this logical connection, it can be seen that what is really central for enhancing student educational outcomes is either to channel students into success (quadrant I) or to steer them away from dropping out (quadrant III) or both. Retention is a necessary but not sufficient condition for student success. Helping students to avoid or overcome barriers is the key to their success, and one way to channel them away from dropping out.

Moreover, as is evident from EMSS assumptions and the associated general model of student success, dropout is included as one of the possible outcomes for students. It is likewise for the various LSSMs discussed in several chapters: Often dropout is one of the outputs of the LSSM concept model. This seems to signal the relevance and importance of dropout as part of the conceptualization of student outcomes. Perhaps a weakness of previous dropout studies is that they did not take into account sufficiently the plurality of outcomes within which dropout takes place. What is needed now is dropout studies that look at the dynamics of dropping out within the broader perspectives provided by well-crafted general models of student success. Alternatively, dropout studies could be done following well-grounded LSSM concept models that are applicable to a specific institution. The latter approach would address the criticism in the research literature that dropout studies have been too general to be useful for practitioners trying to improve student outcomes.

In summary, two points merit further discussion: (1) expecting that well-crafted student (performance) outcome models include both success and dropout as key features of the models and (2) expecting that future research on dropout ought to be guided by either general models of student success or local models of student success. The goal would be to promote greater integration between studies of student success and those devoted to dropout.

Conjugate Models Again

In chapter 1 the importance of scale and complexity were brought into the discussion. In particular, it was noted that theoretical and empirical models of student success are not sufficient to ensure that things are made better for students. These models necessarily exist alongside policy and implementation models that often are left implicit. The disconnection between the various models may be one reason why academic models may be seen as naive views from the ivory tower by those in administrative positions. At the same time, practitioners too often work "from the seat of their pants" as if the problems they are dealing with have not been studied by researchers. This divide between research and practice is deepened when problems and issues are not seen in the broader context of conjugate social arenas that are each guided by their own ends.

Strategies need to be developed that bring together conjugate models from all relevant social arenas so that problems and issues can be understood contextually. This deeply contextualized research would provide the most viable platform for developing action strategies and evaluating the results. But carrying out such research may require rethinking how research is now conducted and organized. The model of a single researcher taking on one problem or issue may have to give way to that of teams of researchers who can collectively develop and articulate all of the conjugate models into one larger metamodel.

Since the various models cut across many disciplines, it also may be necessary to look once again at multidisciplinary research as a driving force to deal with difficult and seemingly intractable problems. One possibility is to organize doctoral students into research teams so that their dissertation work can cover the various conjugate models. Such teams could be organized within one department or across various departments on campus. With the advent of powerful communications technology, collaboration is easier than ever before. It may even be possible to organize virtual research teams across different campuses using advanced communications technology. In this regard, professional associations might be catalysts for bringing together such virtual research teams. All of this has implications for those who provide the funding for research. Should they fund the Lone Ranger model of research, or should they expect researchers finally to pay attention to the complexity of social phenomena and the need to attend to conjugate models? It is time to expand the discussion and to rethink how research can effectively be linked to the life world and the improvement of people's lives.

Are ISSMs the Next Step?

As already pointed out in this book, traditional studies on student dropout and success have tended to focus on results that generalize across various campuses. The emphasis on generalizability across many campuses has resulted in findings that are not particularly applicable to any specific campus and in models that are too general to be useful in the hands of student affairs professionals. EMSS improves on this situation by creating local student success models that can be applied at the individual campus level or even to subpopulations within a given campus. Yet, even the campus or subpopulation levels may be too general when it comes to making sure that every student's chances of succeeding are maximized. Studies such as those by Gandara (1995) show that it is possible to study individual student success. More recently, Colley (2007) investigated the individual success of a handful of Latino students. These and other biographically oriented studies are suggestive of the need to use more powerful theories and techniques to study individual student success. After all, student success occurs one student at a time.

One possibility is to extend the EMSS approach to the individual level. EMSS starts out as a general model of student success (GMSS) that can apply to many campuses and also leads to a local student success model (LSSM) that is applicable at the campus or subpopulation level. The next step would be to develop the methodological tools to create an individual student success model (ISSM) following the general theoretical framework of EMSS. Perhaps a variation of the unfolding matrix could be used. Such a matrix would be completed by an individual student as a means to map the barriers faced by that particular student. Analysis of the matrix data would lead to ISSM taxonomic and concept models. These models in turn would suggest strategic approaches for meeting the needs of a given student. Thus, the ISSM could be a valuable orientation and counseling tool that could be used as part of the freshman year experience. Moreover, the techniques might even be adaptable for assessing the needs of prospective students as they struggle to gain entrance to a postsecondary institution. If well designed, ISSMs might even be useful for parents who want to encourage and help their offspring to succeed. Clearly, ISSMs could be implemented as either scale-free or scaled models. To achieve the latter, instrumentation capable of collecting scaled data would need to be developed. If the development of ISSMs is successful, researchers and practitioners might finally get a glimpse at the microstructure of student success.

The Recovery of Affect

EMSS assumes a rationalist stance that privileges cognition and conation. But anyone who has worked in the student affairs arena knows that the college years are fraught with affective experiences for all students. A close look at the heuristic knowledge that successful students possess often reveals an affective dimension to that knowledge, so it is important to look for ways to include the affective domain in promoting student success. To start, it will be necessary to expand the cognition-conation dyad that currently drives EMSS into a triad of affect, cognition, and conation. Interestingly, the most widely recognized model of student dropout (Tinto's student departure model) is theoretically grounded in the affective domain, given its historic link to Durkheim's theory of suicide and its association with the study of student dropout. What are needed are general models of student success that encompass all aspects of human consciousness, including affect, cognition, and conation. These general models should lead to local student success models and perhaps even individual student success models. Working with tools and models that include the affective domain in addition to the cognitive and conative domains will empower student affairs professionals as they carry out their mission to promote student success.

A New Mission for Student Affairs

Figure 2.3 (chapter 2) clearly demonstrates that student expertise consists of two domains: Academic knowledge and heuristic knowledge. Historically, colleges and universities have recognized these two main divisions of expertise by creating academic affairs and student affairs units. The mission of the academic affairs unit has always been clear: to make sure that students acquire the academic knowledge and skills that are required for graduation. Over many generations, those involved in the academic affairs unit have devoted much time and effort to develop the tools that they need to maximize student achievement in the academic arena.

In the case of heuristic knowledge, the historic picture is not as sanguine. Too often students have been left to their own devices to figure out what constitutes the heuristic knowledge in play and how they might acquire it. The orientation programs typically available to (or even forced on) students are not typically grounded in data-based models of student success. Specific interventions such as freshman seminars, communities of learning, mentoring programs, themed residences, and so on can be seen as attempts to connect students with relevant heuristic knowledge. However, these approaches are not comprehensive, because at best they have an impact on a fraction of the undergraduate population.

EMSS suggests that student affairs units have the opportunity to claim heuristic knowledge as a central focus of their mission. Analogous to that of the academic affairs unit, the mission of student affairs now becomes quite clear: to make sure that students acquire the heuristic knowledge and skills that are required for graduation. Accepting this mission could reenergize student affairs units throughout higher education. There is much work to be done both from a theoretical and from a practical standpoint. For starters, there is the need to develop a pedagogy of heuristic knowledge that strives to develop effective techniques for making heuristic knowledge available to students in a timely and accessible manner. Organizationally, student affairs units need to figure out how to constitute themselves so that they are both service providers and conveyors of heuristic knowledge. Once student affairs is seen as having a fundamental teaching role (i.e., conveying heuristic knowledge) rather than being just a service unit, it will lead to a fundamental rethinking of the organization and staffing of student affairs.

Many challenges also are likely to arise. One important challenge is that, historically, student affairs has not seen itself in a teaching role. Another challenge is that the tools for teaching heuristic knowledge have not yet been well developed. Moreover, thorny issues are likely to arise, such as who is responsible for academic tutoring. One approach is to direct all teaching of academic knowledge to the academic affairs unit and the teaching of heuristic knowledge to the student affairs unit. But the world seldom obeys such simple prescriptions, so it is likely to take a while before good solutions are worked out. What is important is to recognize the great opportunities that EMSS offers to the student affairs profession as it focuses on student success.

AUTOETHNOGRAPHIC ENCOUNTER:
THE PRIMACY OF INVENTION

As I mentioned in chapter 1, my own switch during the mid-1980s from dropout research to student success modeling (SSM) occurred as a result of a fortuitous encounter with Alfredo de los Santos, Jr., who was then struggling with student success issues as a practical concern. I did not know at the time that the switch to SSM would launch me on the path of invention because, as it turned out, I did not have key tools that I needed in order to pursue SSM. At the same time, there was a convergence of sorts that took place. I had been assigned to teach qualitative research methods to doctoral students, and I needed to devote serious effort to understanding how this new field was developing. In addition, since my teenage years I had had a fascination with computers, and the 1980s turned out to be the decade of the "personal computer." So the convergence of these strong currents stimulated me to think in novel and inventive ways.

One day, while wandering around campus, I ran into David Altheide, the symbolic interactionist sociologist. During our brief conversation I asked David if he knew of any software that could be used to analyze qualitative data. As a matter of fact, he said, there was a program called LispQual that had been developed by Chris Drass. I tracked down Chris and asked if I could use the program. It was during the "good ole days" when researchers actually shared software. To my delight, I received from Chris the source code for LispQual, which ran on a mainframe computer—a PDP 11, if I recall correctly. At the time Arizona State University still had a PDP 11, so I went to work installing the program. After a bit of fussing I got it to work. It was quite a feat for me, a rank amateur at programming, especially since I had to learn a bit about LISP (i.e., a list processing language) in order to figure out how Chris had made the program work. Soon personal computers began to take over, and the university wanted to get rid of the PDP 11, so I decided to port LispQual to a personal computer, but using PASCAL instead of LISP (I playfully called the new implementation "PASQUAL"). I actually managed to get the PASCAL version of LispQual to work. The point of all this is that, because I wanted to use computers in the analysis of qualitative data and I also wanted to teach doctoral students how to use the software, finding the right software was key.

At about this time, or soon thereafter, I found out about the Ethnograph, a computer program that John Seidel invented for the analysis of qualitative data and that was based on the IBM PC. I purchased a copy of the program and ran it through its paces. It was good enough so that I made it part of my course on qualitative research methods. Soon the course evolved into Computer Assisted Qualitative Data Analysis, a course that I have been teaching in various guises for over two decades. As it turned out, my students functioned as beta testers for John's program. Whenever the program crashed, I would call John, and he would send a fix right away. Try that with contemporary software!

I taught the Ethnograph for several years and likely would have continued to use it if Apple had not come out with its elegant, graphically oriented user interface on the Macintosh computer. Included with the Macintosh was a program called HyperCard. The Macintosh has always been easy to use but difficult to program. However, the appearance of HyperCard made it possible for just about anyone to get under the hood and program the Macintosh to do something interesting or useful. I immediately saw the potential of using the Macintosh for qualitative data analysis. Previous software had been line oriented, and in order to do any coding the user had to first number the text file line by line and then use these line numbers to get the coding done. It was clear by just looking at the Macintosh that one could and should do coding simply by highlighting with the mouse the desired text and coding that chunk of text. I sat down with my new Macintosh for a few hours, and in that short time I created the first version of HyperQual (the program name is a tip of the hat to Chris Drass). An amended version was released to the public during 1989. The invention of HyperQual allowed me to work more effectively with the analysis of qualitative data in student success modeling.

During the early 1980s my approach to qualitative data analysis was evolving rapidly. I had some reservations about the typical approach then in vogue, in which themes are identified in the data and the presentation of results then consists of extended narratives that liberally quote from the raw data. Influenced by the work of Glaser and Strauss (1967) and others, I became interested in interpretively identifying concepts and documenting them carefully with "exemplars" from the data. A collection of such "grounded concepts" can be seen as the vocabulary one can use to describe and understand a phenomenon. As a bonus, one gets data reduction as concepts are identified.

After a set of grounded concepts is identified, one can look for relationships between the concepts. When these relationships are identified, one has the syntax for relating the concepts. The vocabulary and syntax then provide a language for describing and understanding the phenomenon of interest—a language that is grounded in the phenomenon, with the researcher as interpreter. The presentation of results then takes the form of a graphic concept model of the social situation under investigation, constructed using the concepts and their relationships.

As I was working with these ideas, I became familiar with concept mapping. I liked the idea of concept mapping, but it occurred to me that the cartographic metaphor was too limiting for the range of phenomena that I was interested in studying and the depth of study that I wanted to achieve. As a work-around, I came up with the idea of "concept modeling." It seemed to me that good qualitative research should be able to develop concept models of social situations. Such models could provide insight into social phenomena, but they also could be useful for taking action in the social arena. Over the years, I came to realize that these concept models were scale-free models, and from this vantage point I could then see connections between scale-free and scaled models (for graphical data representation techniques, see Jonassen, Beissner, & Yacci, 1993).

These exciting years taught me that invention is necessary if we are to make progress in understanding things and making them better. While necessity can indeed be seen as the mother of invention, invention itself is the mother of imagined and unimagined futures.

References

Attewell, P., & Lavin, D. E. (2007). *Passing the torch: Does higher education for the disadvantaged pay off across the generations?* New York: Russell Sage Foundation.

Barabasi, A. L. (2003). *Linked.* New York: Penguin Group.

Colley, K. L. (2007). *Latino success stories in higher education: A qualitative study of recent graduates from a health science center.* Unpublished doctoral dissertation, University of North Texas.

Gandara, P. C. (1995). *Over the ivy walls: The educational mobility of low-income Chicanos*. Albany: State University of New York Press.

Glaser, B., & Strauss, A. (1967). *The discovery of grounded theory: Strategies for qualitative research*. Chicago: Aldine.

Jonassen, D. H., Beissner, K., & Yacci, M. (1993). Structural knowledge: Techniques for representing, conveying, and acquiring structural knowledge. Hillsdale, NJ: Erlbaum.

Zeidenberg, M., Jenkins, D., & Calcagno, J. C. (2007, June). *Do student success courses actually help community college students succeed?* (CCRC Brief No. 36). New York: Columbia University, Community College Research Center.

CONTRIBUTORS

Kimberly S. Barker is an assistant professor at Texas A&M University-Kingsville, System Center San Antonio. She is currently working in the College of Education, Department of Curriculum and Instruction.

Mary J. Miller is the Instructional Compliance Director for the Edgewood Independent School District in San Antonio, Texas. Prior to this appointment, she served as an elementary school principal for ten years.

George E. Norton is the Assistant Vice President of Student Affairs for Admissions, Orientation & Transition Services at The University of Texas at San Antonio.

Raymond V. Padilla is a professor in the Department of Educational Leadership and Policy Studies at the University of Texas at San Antonio.

Ralph Mario Wirth is an administrator and director of educational planning at The San Antonio School for Inquiry and Creativity, as well as lead researcher for the Democratic Schools Research Institute, Inc.